TRADITIONAL SCOTTISH DY.

CW01464922

# TRADITIONAL SCOTTISH DYES

and how to make them

## Jean Fraser

*Illustrated by Florence Knowles*

CANONGATE

First published 1983
by
Canongate Publishing Ltd
17 Jeffrey Street
Edinburgh Scotland


Revised edition 1985
Reprinted 1988

© 1983,1985 Jean Fraser
© illustrations 1983, 1985 Florence Knowles


*All rights reserved*

Fraser, Jean, *1922* —
Traditional Scottish dyes: and how to make them.
— 2nd ed.
1. Dyes and dyeing — Wool — Amateurs' manuals
I. Title
677'.331          TP899
ISBN 0 86241 108 4


Typeset by Witwell Ltd, Liverpool
Printed & bound by The Bath Press, Great Britain

# CONTENTS

# Introduction &
# Acknowledgements

Dyeing with plants is an intriguing craft, and Scotland with its tradition of famous tweeds and tartans is one of the countries for which it is still renowned.

In the past, dyeing methods were jealously guarded secrets normally handed down by word of mouth from one generation to the next, hence very few were in fact recorded. Dyeing was a form of self expression which enabled women to dress their families a little bit differently from their neighbours; but alas, today only a very few of the older generation continue to use this traditional family craft; and it is this which has inspired me to search out and gather together the old dyeing recipes before they too vanish, as have so many other traditions of the Highlands and Islands.

Natural dye colours are obtained from roots, berries, bark, leaves and lichen (or crottle). The colours themselves vary greatly, depending as they do on the geology of the area and on plant distribution, which, inevitably, had a considerable influence on the make-up of the early tartans and tweeds. Indeed, dyers in neighbouring glens often got different results from the same plant according to the minerals in their respective water supplies.

In 1783 the ban on the wearing of tartans was lifted, and in addition a wider range of foreign vegetable dyestuffs of greater strength and simpler application began to be imported into Scotland, with the result that some recipes from earlier times stopped being used and were soon forgotten. Even by 1700 indigo is reported as having been regularly shipped to St Kilda, and as far back as the sixteenth century, consignments of wool were being sent to Holland to be dyed a particular scarlet.

In 1841 Mr T. Edmonston Jun., Balta Sound, Shetland, read a paper on the native dyes of the Shetland Islands to the Botanical Society of Edinburgh. He remarks that the dyes used in Shetland were, in former times, derived entirely from native plants; lately however madder, indigo, and logwood had been imported and widely used. Many beautiful dyes were said to have been known to our

1

ancestors, but which are now lost to us. Writing of his own time he says that the only colours made were brown, red, yellow and black and that the cloth dyed is usually very coarse and takes the colour easily.

But the great event which changed the whole face of dyeing world-wide, was the discovery of synthetic Aniline dyes at the end of the 1800's which were derived from coal tar and gave harsher but stronger colours. They were also labour saving and cheap. Colour matching too was easier and more reliable. They became increasingly available with the inevitable result that they soon became the universal dyestuff. The impact on natural dyeing was predictable; it fell into immediate decline, almost to the point of extinction, and with this many of the old traditional recipes disappeared too. But for all its versatility, an Aniline dye just cannot match the delicacy and lustre of its natural counterpart, even in spite of its unpredictable colour matching. A typical example of this may be found in Persian carpets where colour variation often appears for no particular reason in the pattern. This is because the weavers ran out of colour and could not match it exactly in the next batch of dyeing. This does not detract from the quality of the finished article. On the contrary, it is a sure mark of authenticity. Indeed natural dyed carpets are in great demand, as is naturally dyed cloth.

Happily in recent years there has been a welcome resurgence of interest in natural dyes, in spite of the almost primitive image of Highland women spinning outside their crofts. Indeed, dyeing is a simple craft which can be fun and yet does not require much skill. The wool used can be for knitting, crochet, embroidery, spinning or weaving. I myself spin and then weave or knit the yarn after I have dyed it. Exact amounts of wool and dyestuff can vary each time you use them and then results will be different – in fact it is often difficult to get exactly the same shade again. It may be, for instance, that a robust plant has been used or has been growing in the shade. These are the sort of things that affect the colour.

Most important of all is that one gains through one's experience and trial and error. This is why dyeing with natural dyestuff is so intriguingly individual and of course explains why in the old days the women were so loath to disclose their own recipes. It also explains why it would be misleading to put precise instructions on all recipes.

The recipes in this book are meant to help groups or individuals with simple experiments. Inevitably the list of recipes is incomplete by the very nature of the task I have set myself. For instance, I have not been able to find any recipes for bitter vetch, marsh cinquefoil, monk's rhubarb or teasel, although each of them has been mentioned as having been used in dyeing. A list of my reference sources may be found at the end of the book.

Surprisingly little has been written down because the women who did their own dyeing were very secretive. I even came across an example of this in present times when I was told that the recipes, safe in a chest in the Western Isles, were to be burnt when the owner died and not passed on to the next generation! Sources like the Scottish Home Industries and a foreman from the Tweed Mill in Portree in 1922 are responsible for a considerable amount of information, but as they were not dyers themselves they were only reporting what they believed the recipes to be.

Some recipes have come from individuals and to these people I am very grateful and acknowledge their help with many thanks; Miss Marian Campbell of Harris, Mr Duncan McColl of Oban, Mrs Alex MacDonald of Harris, Mr R Haggerty of Benbecula, Miss Chrissie MacGillivray of Mull and Mrs Barr of Callander. I should be most grateful if any additional recipes are known and could be sent to me to complete the record.

And now I want to pay a special tribute to Mrs Florence Knowles of Moniack Bridge, Inverness for her drawings. These are exquisite, both in their detail and design, and set off the book to perfection. My very grateful thanks to her.

I hope this book will encourage all those who use it to experiment and to enjoy it. Whatever the result, it will be interesting, often lovely, and always your very own work.

*Jean Fraser 1983*

# Equipment

A sink with hot and cold water
A domestic cooker
A pair of scales
Note book
Label tags
Pencil
Mordants: see page 8 for details
Cream of tartar
Salt
Washing soda
Baking soda
Vinegar
Soap flakes
Ammonia
Plant material
Wool
Old stockings or tights

The following items MUST BE KEPT ONLY FOR DYEING:
1 stainless steel or enamel pan and 1 medium size enamel pan (called dyebaths in recipes)
Iron pot (to be used only when specified) – optional
Wooden spoon
sharp knife
Measuring cup
Glass jars
A cooking thermometer – optional
Sieve or collender
Rubber gloves

Group work:
Blackboard
Bunsen burners (use with caution)

# Collecting Plant Material

The collection of plant material for dyeing should be done with the greatest care, with conservation of plant life always in mind. Ingredients may grow prolifically but this is no excuse for picking every piece in sight. Use your discretion and be a responsible member of the countryside. This applies particularly to Lichen/Crottles, some of which take a lifetime to grow only one inch. Pollution from towns travels far and is destroying them, so they are something to be treasured.

Care must be taken to pick when the plant needed is 'ready', that is, when most of the dye producing substances are concentrated in the part you want to collect.

## Spring
Young shoots can be gathered in early growth.

## Summer
Throughout spring and summer there will be leaves and flowers to use fresh. Plants such as heather flowers and crottle may be dried and kept for later use. Bark can be collected and where possible find a tree or branch recently felled and take the bark from there. Be very careful not to kill trees by taking too much bark off one area or one particular tree.

## Autumn
Berries, roots and crottle can be collected.

When collecting roots never take tap roots or damage the root system to such an extent that the tree or bush would die as a result. Naturally you should replace any earth you have to remove.

The time of collection will affect the colours achieved as will the location of the plant in relation to sunlight, rain, soil and seasonal weather conditions. All these factors contribute to the character of the plant and therefore to the colours achieved in dyeing. Each time you dye with vegetable materials it is an experiment because every collection of plants is unique. Repeated use of the same dyestuff will prove how varied the results can be.

# Imported Dyestuffs

Indigo, Logwood, Cochineal and Madder were imported and widely used.

# Wool

Most natural dyes yield more brilliant and lasting colours if used with wool. Due to the substances in its cell walls, the molecules of the mordants and dyes are bound more easily to it than to the celluloid constituents of plant fibres. If possible, natural unbleached wool should be used. The yarn should be tied into small skeins about ½ oz dry weight. They require a minimum of plant material and only about a quart or so of dyebath solution, and good colour samples can be obtained with this amount. You can obtain unbleached wool from:

T. M. Hunter Limited  
Brora  
Sutherland KW9 6NA  
Scotland

Craftman's Mark Limited  
Tone Dale Mill  
Wellington  
Somerset TA21 0AW

If you wish to dye the wool in the fleece and then spin it, you will find your local Wool Marketing Board a good source of supply. Any wool used for dyeing must first be washed in warm water with good soap flakes, steeping it and moving it lightly in plenty of water rather than real washing and squeezing, as this would matt the wool. Rinse in water of the same temperature. Rain water is ideal for this purpose. If dyeing wool in the fleece and after it has been washed, it may be put in a net bag or old nylon stockings (do not pack it too tightly). This prevents dyestuffs getting tangled in the wool.

To make a skein quickly, and be sure to tie the two ends by loosely taking the thread in two half hitches and knotting it securely to the last hitch of wool. Additional loose cotton ties can be added if desired, as they help to keep the skeins from getting tangled and allow the dye to penetrate.

The "Romantic Story of the Highland Garb and the Tartan" says "The process of washing was to wash the thread thoroughly with liquid ammonia (probably stale urine) then rinse well in cold water and put in to the pot . . .", while Provost Ross in the Scottish Home Industries report of 1895 says ". . . wash the thread thoroughly in Lye (Gaelic, *maighstir*) then . . . rinse and wash it in pure water and put it into the pot of dye". Lye is water alkanized by lixiviation of vegetable ashes – a strong alkaline solution especially for washing.

"In olden times in some parts of the country the wool was first spun and then dyed in the hank or skein. Usually the wool was put in the cauldron [iron], a very large one, with a layer of wool and with a layer of the dye plant alternately and the cauldron filled up with water and the desired mordant added. This might be in layers too. In some cases the plant was boiled in the water first, then removed and the wool already mordanted was dyed in the resulting water."

# Mordanting or colour fixing

Preparing the wool that has already been washed. The word 'mordant' derives from the Latin 'mordere' meaning to bite, and refers to any substance applied for the purpose of fixing the colour. Mordanting is generally essential if the dye is to 'take' properly and remain permanent. It also enriches the colour. Mordants most frequently used are the metallic salts of Alum, Chrome, Iron and Tin.

*Important* – some of these chemicals are harmful and all should be labelled POISON and kept away from children.

Alum can be bought at any chemist and is the mordant most frequently used. The other chemicals would have to be ordered from a special firm such as:
1. The Textile Workshop and Gallery, 166 High Street, Edinburgh EH1 1QS
2. London Textiles Workshop, 65 Roseberry Road, London N10

*Alum* (Potassium Aluminium Sulphate). This is the most commonly used of all the mordants. It is sometimes used in combination with Cream of Tartar, as this brightens and evens the colour. To mordant wool with Alum use:

|  | |
|---|---|
| | 4 oz Alum to 1 lb of coarse strong wool |
| varying to: | 3 oz Alum to 1 lb of fine wool |
| | Use 1 oz Cream of Tartar to every 4 oz Alum |

**Method**: Dissolve the Alum, and when necessary, the Cream of Tartar and add it to the pan of water. There should be enough water to cover the wool generously and allow for free circulation. Put the pan over the heat and stir well. As the water begins to get warm, add the wet and washed wool and bring the temperature up gradually until it reaches boiling point. Allow to simmer one hour for coarse wool, or about ¾ hour for finer wool. The mordanting is then finished. Lift the wool out of the pan with a wooden spoon and let it drain a moment. Squeeze the excess water gently out of it, but do not wring it, or wash it. The wool may be dyed immediately, but it is better left a day or two. Dry in the shade hanging the skein over a stick, or on plain paper in an airing cupboard.

An historical note mentions that Fir Club Moss was used specifically in place of Alum in Scotland. No quantities were mentioned but it grows on mountains in damp places and experiments could be tried.

*Chrome* (Potassium Dichromate). This is a very useful mordant as it gives the wool a soft and silky feel. A lid should be kept on the pan of this mordant as it is very sensitive to light and the dye may be uneven if this is not done. For the same reason, if you want to store the wool, it must be put wet into a black plastic bag. It can only be kept like this for a week or two. To mordant wool with Chrome use:

$\frac{1}{4}$ – $\frac{1}{2}$oz Chrome to 1lb wool

*Method* Dissolve the Chrome with boiling water in a cup and add it to the pan of water. There should be enough water to cover the wool generously and allow for free circulation. Put in the washed, wetted wool and slowly bring up to simmering point. Simmer for 1 to $1\frac{1}{2}$ hours for coarse wool, or $\frac{3}{4}$ to 1 hour for fine wool. Stir carefully from time to time always being careful to replace the lid. You may either use it straight away or keep it in a black plastic bag.

Recipes from Portree in this book appear to combine Chrome and the dyestuff together in one operation. Chrome dissolves easily and I often add it directly to the dyebath without first dissolving it in a cup.

# Mordants used during the Dyeing Process

*Tin* (Stannous Chloride). This is chiefly used when very bright shades of red and yellow are required for the wool. It is sometimes used as a mordant or put into the dyebath towards the end of dyeing so as to brighten the colour. The recipes in this book only use it in the latter way.

$\frac{1}{2}$oz Tin crystals
2oz Cream of Tartar     to 1lb wool

For $\frac{1}{2}$oz skeins of wool, use enough of the crystals to cover a $\frac{1}{2}$p piece.

**Method:** After the wool has been simmered for the required time, lift it out with a wooden spoon and stir the Cream of Tartar into the dyebath. Dissolve the Tin in a cup with some boiling water before adding it to the dyebath. Stir well with a wooden spoon and return the wool. Simmer for $\frac{1}{4}$ hour stirring occasionally. Take the wool out and wash it in hot soapy water of a similar temperature to the dyebath, cool and rinse. Dry over a stick hanging in the shade.

*Iron* (Ferrous Sulphate or Copperas). This is rather a difficult mordant to use as wool mordanted with Iron is apt to dye unevenly. The easiest method with which to get a very slight Iron mordant is to use an old iron pot. This was frequently used by the Scottish dyers. Iron tends to darken and dull colours and change yellows into greens. If an iron pot is not available use:

$\frac{1}{2}$oz Iron
1oz Cream of Tartar     to 1lb wool

For $\frac{1}{2}$oz skeins of wool, use enough to cover a $\frac{1}{2}$p piece.

**Method:** Simmer the wool for the required time in the dyebath. If necessary take out the dyestuff. Dissolve the Iron and Cream of Tartar in a cup of boiling water and add them to the dyebath. Stir well and then add the wetted wool and simmer for 20 – 40 minutes according to the colour required. Stir occasionally. This is sometimes called a 'saddening process'. Rinse very thoroughly after mordanting with Iron. Dry over a stick hanging in the shade.

In Scotland, Iron mordanting was evidently obtained from certain black bogs and in Shetland cloth was sometimes rubbed over with Iron Ore before dyeing.

*Copper Sulphate* (Blue Vitriol). This is a mordant which has to be used very sparingly as it is inclined to rot the wool.

½oz to every 1lb wool

**Method**: After the wool has been simmered for the required time (dyeing) in the dyebath, lift it out and put in the Copper Sulphate. This will take some time to dissolve so stir well and do not add the wool until you are sure it has dissolved. Cool the dyebath and then put back the wool and simmer for an hour. Rinse well and dry.

*Common Salt* (Sodium Chloride). Used to set any blue/violet dye obtained from berries.

1 tablespoon to 1 pint

## Points to remember in Mordanting

1. Use a large enough pot.
2. Have enough water to circulate round the wool evenly.
3. Stir occasionally with a wooden spoon. Too much stirring will felt the wool.
4. Make sure the mordant is dissolved before adding the water.
5. Skeins must not be tied too tight.
6. Too much Alum makes the wool rather sticky.
7. Too much Chrome spoils the colour.
8. Too much Tin makes it harsh and brittle.
9. Too much Iron hardens the wool.

## Storing and Labelling of Mordanted Wool

Wool mordanted with Alum will keep indefinitely after it is dried. Dry over a stick in the shade and put in a bag labelled

"Wool mordanted with Alum". It is best to keep it for 24 hours after it is mordanted and before it is used for dyeing. Wool mordanted with Chrome can be kept wet in a black plastic bag for one or two weeks. Label the bag "wool mordanted with Chrome".

# General Instructions for Dyeing

It is essential that all wool is mordanted before the dyeing process begins. See each individual recipe for the type of mordant needed. When the dyestuff is substantive this means it needs no mordant.

There is a choice of two ways of dyeing; this is governed by the substance of the dye material used:

(a) The skeins of wool ready mordanted may be put in layers in amongst the plant material.

(b) The dyestuff is boiled. Then when ready the liquid is strained into the dyebath (or saucepan) and the wool added when the liquid has cooled. Alternatively, put the dyestuff in a net or old nylon tights and take out of the dyebath when the dye has been extracted.

Recipes in this book indicate which method is used.

**Method:**

1. Be sure the skeins are correctly tied in two or three places before mordanting or dyeing. Each skein should weigh about ½oz in dry weight. They require a minimum of plant material and only about a quart or so of dyebath solution, and good colour samples can be obtained with this amount.

2. Weigh the plant material and take the same weight in dry wool. Place it in an enamel or stainless steel pan. (Aluminium and iron pots alter the colour slightly, ie Aluminium dulls the colour and Iron will turn yellow dye a greenish shade.) Cover the layers of plant material and wetted mordanted wool with cold water.

3. Heat slowly till just below boiling-point and simmer for the required time.

4. If you wish to combine additional mordants as alterants (see next chapter) this is the time to do so. First take out the wool and be sure to dissolve the mordant separately in hot water and then stir it into the solution before the wool is added again. It is possible to dye the skeins of wool prepared with different mordants in the same dyebath.

13

5. Use a wooden spoon and remove the skein of wool when it is the colour you want.

6. *Either* allow to cool and then rinse in cold water *or* you must rinse in the same temperature as the dyebath. If this is not done you will shock and felt the wool. This method applies to both alternative ways of dyeing.

7. Labels should be clearly written giving material used, date when picked, mordant or alterants used, and be put on the appropriate skein immediately.

   Notebooks should have a sample of wool stuck in with glue beside the recipe, or wool can be threaded through a punched hole at the edge of the page. The full recipe should be written down giving details as on the label, plus length of simmering in the dyebath, where the material used was found and date.

8. To dry the skeins of wool, loop over a smooth stick and hang in the shade, or put on plain paper in an airing cupboard.

9. Exhaust baths. The first batch of dyeing will seldom exhaust the dye substance in the dyebath and therefore a fresh batch of wool may be entered in the same manner as the first and this will give a weaker colour. Sometimes there may be a second and third dyeing. If wished the solution can be kept in a glass screwtop jar for use at a later date. Remember to label the jar.

# Alterants

Alterants are chemical solutions used if colour changes are required once the initial dyeing has been done.

*Ammonia* In the old days before Ammonia was available in commercial form, the dyers used urine which of course contains Ammonia. It was called 'fual' or 'graith' in the Gaelic, and many households collected it in a barrel or tub. They probably did not know why they used it, but they certainly knew what the results would be. In "History of Highland Dress" John Telfer Dunbar says "Urine was used in many recipes where deep shades were required. Fuller rather than darker colours are implied and it served to intensify the colour helping to extract the greatest possible amount of dyestuff from the plant". It was used in the fermentation of lichens to make the Cudbear dye and also with Indigo.

Modern experiments in the use of Ammonia solution show that colours can be:

(a) Deepened or intensified;
(b) Lightened;
(c) Completely changed to a different colour.

Use one part of Scrubbs Ammonia to three parts water.

The most dramatic changes occur in the pink/lilac shade range, which, after an ammonia wash frequently change to various shades of green, the extent of such change being dependent on:

(a) The original dyed shade;
(b) the strength of the Ammonia, and
(c) the duration of immersion in the Ammonia bath.

Shades of green have been obtained in this way from Elderberries, Blackberries and Blaeberries.

Chemically, these changes appear to be related to the fact that some natural dyes are PH indicators, the most well known being the Lichen (Rocella Montagnei) which is used in the manufacture of litmus paper. An alkaline solution (PH>7) changes the litmus paper to blue, while an acid solution (PH<7) changes it to red. Similar colour reactions to a change in PH occur in other natural dye pigments.

*Acetic Acid* (Vinegar). Used to acidify a dyebath solution in order to neutralise alkaline water, and as a solvent for colouring matter. Vinegar itself may be used when added to some recipes after dyeing is completed. It gives another tone or shade. (Ordinary Vinegar is 3 – 6% so one part of 30% acetic acid equals ten parts of weak Vinegar.)

*Washing Soda* This is used in the same way as Vinegar and brings out the blue tones in Cudbear.

*Rowan Berries* These were used as an additive to madder and cochineal to give very bright colours.

# Colours – Which plants to collect

The chart below gives all the plants that produce a particular colour. Choose the plant for the colour you require according to the time of year and the plant's availability. On page 5 you will see the best time of year for picking the various plants.

All the plants have their own recipes which can be found in alphabetical order. As a general rule, the plants in italics are the easiest to find and the most practical to use.

## YELLOW

Alder    Ash    Bearberry    *Birch*
Bog Myrtle    Broom
*Corn Marigold*    *Cow Parsley*    *Crab Apple*
*Crottle Evernia Prunastri*    Dock    Elder    *Heather*
*Knapweed*    Marsh Marigold    Marsh Woundwort
Meadow Sweet    *Nettles*
Polyganum Hydropiper    Polyganum Persicaria
*Poplar*    *Ragwort*    *Whin*    Weld    *Yarrow*

---

## GREEN

*Birch*    Blaeberry    *Bog Myrtle*    *Bracken*
Bog Bean    Broom    *Coltsfoot*    *Cow Parsley*
*Elder*    *Heather*    Ivy    Knapweed    *Nettles*
*Onion Skins*    Privet    Ragwort    Reed    Rush
Thistle    Whin    Weld

---

## BROWN

Blaeberry    *Crottle*    *Black Crottle*    Red Currant
Dulse    Heather    Juniper    Knapweed    Oak
Peat Soot    Poplar    *Ragwort*    Reindeer Moss
Sea Ivory    *Sorrel*    *Tansy*

---

## PURPLE

Birch Bark    Blaeberry    *Bramble*    *Cudbear*
Crottle Xanthoria Parientina

## BLACK

Dock     Dog Rose     Hawthorn     Meadow Sweet
Poplar     Water Lily Roots     Willow

---

## RED

Black Thorn Bark     Bramble     *Cudbear*
Lady's Bedstraw     St. John's Wort     Tormentil

---

## ORANGE

Barberry     *Bog Myrtle*     *Onion Skins*     *Heather*

---

## PINK

*Bramble*     *Lady's Bedstraw*
*Crottle Xanthoria Parientina*     Willow

---

## GREY/BLUE/VIOLET

*Blackthorn*     *Blaeberry*     *Bramble*     *Cudbear*
Crottle Xanthoria Parientina     Elder     Elecampane
Iris

# The Recipes

The recipes in this book are meant to help groups or individuals with simple experiments in old Scottish dyeing methods. The information also acts as a record of what recipes are available on the subject in the present day; on the other hand recipes for Bitter Vetch, Marsh Cinquefoil, Monk's Rhubarb and Teasel cannot now be found, though the plants are mentioned as having been used in dyeing. This is why I have sometimes included skeleton recipes to act as a record. To give additional interest, notes on other uses of the plants have also been given.

Each plant is listed alphabetically with a special section on Crottle/Lichen giving some of the varieties used. A Table may be found on the previous pages as a guide to the colours that may be obtained. The plants printed in italics are those which are fairly easily available and simple to use, and therefore suitable for beginners and group work. It must be remembered though, as mentioned under the heading "Collecting the Plant Material" that there is a special time and season for collecting the various items used in dyeing. The different colours mentioned as being obtained from one plant are produced by using different mordants or colour fixing agents and sometimes different parts of the plant, i.e. roots or flowering tips.

# 1. Alder

(Alnus Glutinosa)
(Gael. Fearna)

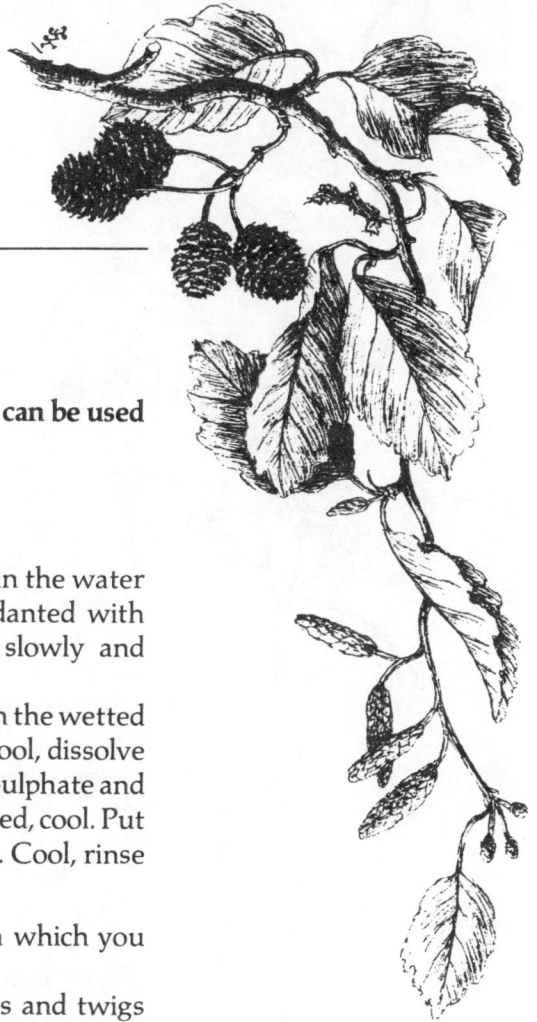

**The bark should be collected in the Summer. It can be used fresh or dried.**

1. Black
Use 2lbs bark to 1lb wool
*Method* Chop up the bark and soak it overnight in the water to be used for dyeing. Use wool already mordanted with Alum and Cream of Tartar. Heat the bark slowly and simmer for about two hours.
Strain the liquid into the dyebath and cool. Put in the wetted wool and simmer for 1½ hours. Take out the wool, dissolve carefully in the dyebath ½ teaspoonful Copper Sulphate and one teaspoonful Iron. Stir well and when dissolved, cool. Put in the wool and simmer for a further 1½ hours. Cool, rinse well and dry.

2. Here is an interesting recipe from Jura with which you could experiment.
*Method* A large pot was filled with Alder leaves and twigs from which a black dye was obtained by a simple infusion as with tea and the colour was made fast by the addition of Logwood and Iron.

3. Brown
*Method* Follow recipe No. 1 for black, until you take out the wool after simmering 1½ hours, then put in ½ teaspoonful of Chrome, dissolve well, cool and add the wool for a further ½ hour simmering and stirring occasionally, also remembering to put on a lid. Cool, rinse well and dry.

*Other uses*
The bark when steeped in hot water produces a tonic and gargle for sore throat. The mixture has also been used as an astringent.

21

# 2. Alder Buckthorn

*(Frangula Alnus)*
*(Gael. Ramh Droighionn)*

### 1. Black
Use 2lbs bark to 1lb wool
*Method* Chop up the bark and soak it overnight in the water you will use for dyeing. Use wool already mordanted with Alum and Cream of Tartar. Heat the bark slowly and simmer for two hours. Strain the liquid into the dyebath and cool. Add the wetted wool and simmer for ½ hour, stirring occasionally. Take out the wool and allow to cool. Rinse and dry.

### 2. Yellow
Use 2lbs bark and leaves mixed to 1lb wool
*Method* Take wool mordanted with Alum and Cream of Tartar and cover the leaves, bark and wool with cold water. Simmer for 1½ hours, stirring occasionally. Take out the wool, cool, rinse and dry.

### 3. Green and Blue/Grey
It is reported that a good green can be obtained from the unripe berries and a blue/grey from ripe berries. No recipes available.

# 3. Barberry

*(Berberis vulgaris)*
*(Gael. Geur-dhearc or Barbrag)*

**A shrub, probably introduced; occasionally found wild in hedges, often grown in gardens for ornament.**
**This is a substantive dye and needs no mordant.**

1. Orange
*Method* Cut up the stems with a sharp knife and cover with cold water and boil for two hours. Pour liquid into the dyebath and cool. Add the wetted wool and simmer for ½ hour. Cool and rinse.

In Portree Barberry root is also reported to have been used.

2. Green
Dr Maclagan 1898 reported getting green from the root. No mordant was mentioned but the use of Alum and Iron is suggested.

# 4. Bear-berry

*(Arctostaphylos)*
*(Gael. Grainnseag)*

**The whole plant (except the root) of this trailing under-shrub of the Highlands can be used all the year. It fruits July-September and is best picked before the berries form. Use 1lb plant material to 1lb wool.**

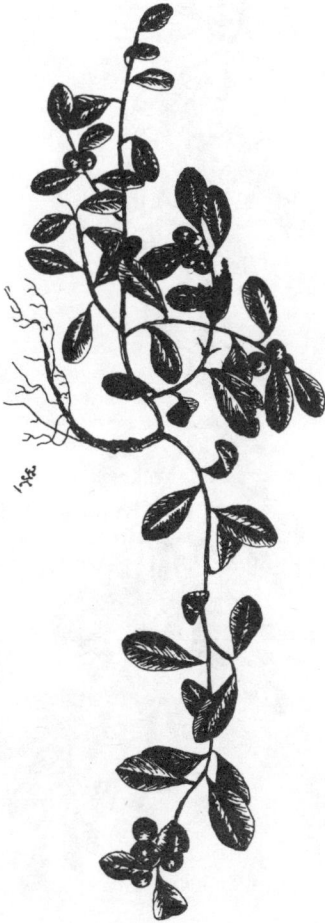

1. Yellow Green
*Method* Cover the plant material with cold water and boil for two hours and strain the liquid into the dyebath. Cool and add the wetted wool mordanted with Alum and Cream of Tartar pushing it down with a wooden spoon. Simmer for half an hour stirring occasionally then lift out the wool and cool. Rinse and dry.

2. Blue Green
*Method* As in recipe No 1 but after simmering for ½ an hour take out the wool and add a little Copper Sulphate to the dyebath.
When dissolved put back the wool and simmer for a further ½ an hour stirring occasionally. Lift out the wool and cool, rinse and dry.

3. Blue/Black
*Method* 1lb berries to 1lb wool
Cover the berries with cold water and add the wetted wool mordanted with Alum and Cream of Tartar. Bring to boil and simmer ¾ hour stirring occasionally. Lift out the wool and cool. Rinse and dry.

*Other uses*
Badge of the Colquhouns.
The leaves were used as a tonic for troubles of the bladder and for stone and gravel cures.
The plant was used by Highlanders long ago for tanning leather.
The berries of this plant are not eaten.

# 5. Birch

---

*(Betula Alba)*
*(Gael. Beithe. Beithe Beag)*

**BIRCH, DWARF (Betula Nana) For a brighter yellow use the dwarf birch. Charles Fergusson in his book "The Gaelic Names of Trees, Shrubs and Plants" 1878, says "The leaves and twigs of this variety yield a much brighter yellow dye than any other varieties of birch and is much sought after by Highland housewives."**

1. Yellow
Use 2lbs leaves to 1lb wool – if dried, double quantity necessary.
*Method* Put the leaves into cold water and soak overnight in the water for dyeing, add the wet Alum and Cream of Tartar mordanted wool. Bring up to simmering point slowly and simmer about one hour, stirring occasionally so as to get an even dye. Take the wool out with a wooden spoon, cool, rinse and dry in the shade.

# 6. Birch Bark

*(Gael. Beatha)*

1. Red/Purple
Use 1lb bark to ½lb wool

*Method* Steep the inner bark overnight in the water to be used for dyeing. Heat slowly and simmer two hours. Strain off the liquid into a dyebath, cool a little and enter wetted Alum and Cream of Tartar mordanted wool. Simmer for about 1½ hours stirring with a wooden spoon occasionally. Take out the wool and dissolve a little Cream of Tartar in the dyebath and then dissolve a little iron in a cup with boiling water before adding it to the dyebath. Stir. Put in the wool and stir occasionally for 20 minutes. Cool, rinse well and dry.

2. Green
*Method* Using the bark as in recipe No. 1 and after it has simmered for two hours, add 2oz of Copper Sulphate. Stir until dissolved. Cool. Enter wetted mordanted wool and simmer for one hour. Cool, rinse well and dry.

# 7. Blackthorn

*(Prunus Spinosa)*
*(Gael. Airne. Preas nan airneag)*

## 1. Rose Pink
1lb well bruised berries to 1lb wool
*Method* Cover the sloes and Alum and Cream of Tartar mordanted wool with cold water and bring up to simmer for one hour. Stir occasionally to get an even dye. Lift out the wool. Cool, rinse and dry.

## 2. Grey/Blue
*Method* As in recipe No. 1 but at the end lift out the wool and put it into a hot solution of ready dissolved soap flakes. Take it out after a few minutes and cool, rinse and dry.

## 3. Red/Brown
Use 2lbs bark to 1lb wool
*Method* Soak the bark overnight in the water you will use for dyeing. Strain off the liquid into the dyebath. Add a little Chrome to the dyebath. Stir to dissolve it. Cool. Add the wetted wool. Simmer until the required shade. Cool, rinse and dry.

## 4. Orange
*Method* As above in recipe No. 3 but this time use Alum and Cream of Tartar mordanted wool and no Chrome. Simmer till the required shade. Cool, rinse and dry.

# 8. Blaeberry

*(Vaccinium Myrtillus)*
*(Gael. Lus nan Dearc, Lus nan Braoileag)*

## 1. Purple
Use 1lb well bruised berries to 1lb wool
*Method* Crush the berries in the dyebath and add some soft water to cover – rain water would do. Enter the wetted Alum and Cream of Tartar mordanted wool and push it down among the berries with a wooden spoon. Simmer slowly stirring occasionally for one hour or longer till the colour is obtained. Lift out the wool with a wooden spoon. Cool, rinse and dry.

## 2. Blue
*Method* As for recipe No. 1 but after the wool has simmered for one hour, take out the wool and dissolve a little Cream of Tartar in the dyebath and then dissolve 1 teaspoonful Iron in a cup of boiling water, add this to the dyebath and stir. Cool. Put in the wool and simmer 15 minutes. Take out the wool, cool and rinse well in salted water. An iron pot could be used in this recipe in which case leave out the Iron mordant.

## 3. Violet
*Method* A Portree recipe says the thread was washed in Ammonia before dyeing as in recipe No. 1.

## 4. Brown
*Method* As for recipe No. 1 and simmer the wool for one hour. Add a handful or two of oak apples. Simmer for a further hour, stirring occasionally. Lift out the wool with a wooden spoon, cool, rinse and dry.

## 5. Sage Green
*Method* As for recipe No. 1 and when a purple colour is achieved, take out the wool and add a 10% solution of Ammonia and stir well and return the wool. Simmer until a sage green, stirring occasionally. Take out the wool, cool, rinse and dry. (Scrubb's Ammonia is about 10%).

*Other uses*
In Arran and the Western Isles they are given for diarrhoeas and dysentries with good effect. The Highlanders frequently eat them in milk, which is a cooling agreeable food, and sometimes they make them into tarts and jellies, which they mix with whisky to give it a relish to strangers.

# 9. Bog Bean

*(Menyanthaceae Trifoliata)*
*(Gael. Ponair Chapull)*

**BUCK BEAN, MARSH TREFOIL Found on the edge of lochs and streams. This recipe was sent to me by Ruariadh Haggerty, one of the few people with knowledge of dyeing on the island of Benbecula.**

1. Ancient Green
Young heather tips were boiled to produce Ancient Green in common with Bog Bean. No mordant was mentioned, but it is suggested that Alum and Cream of Tartar should be tried.

*Other uses*
A tea made from the dried leaves relieves headaches and migraine.

# 10. Bog Myrtle

*(Myrica Gale)*
*(Gael. Roid)*

## 1. Yellow
Use 1lb leaves to 1lb wool
*Method* If you use the leaves dried they need soaking overnight in cold water which can then be used for the dyeing process. If the leaves are fresh put them in cold water. Add the wetted Cream of Tartar and Alum mordanted wool and, with a wooden spoon, push it down amongst the leaves. Bring up to simmer slowly and simmer until you get the desired colour – probably ½ hour, stirring occasionally. Take out and cool, rinse and dry.

## 2. Yellow Brown
*Method* As for recipe No. 1 but take out the wool when the yellow colour is achieved. Add a little Copper Sulphate, stir well to dissolve then put back the wool for a further 20 minutes simmering and stir. Take it out. Cool, rinse well and dry.

## 3. Orange
*Method* As for recipe No. 1 but take out the wool when the yellow colour is achieved. Dissolve a little Cream of Tartar in the dyebath and then dissolve a little Tin in a cup of boiling water. Add to the dyebath and stir. Return the wool for a further 20 minutes simmering. Take it out with a wooden spoon and wash in a hot soapy water the same temperature as the dyebath. Cool, rinse and dry.

## 4. Yellow Green
*Method* As for recipe No. 1 but take out when the yellow colour is achieved. Lift out the wool and dissolve a little Cream of Tartar in the dyebath and then dissolve a little Iron in a cup of boiling water, add it to the dyebath and stir well. Return the wool and simmer for 20 minutes and stir. Take out the wool. Cool, rinse and dry. An iron pot could be used in this recipe and so leaving out the Iron mordant.

*Other uses*

Highlanders slept on beds of Bog Myrtle which is flea-proof. Bog Myrtle was also put among linen to repel moths. Long before hops, the plant was used to flavour beer. Scouts were taught to bruise the fragrant leaves in their tents to discourage insects. Bog Myrtle was used in the process of tanning. The cones boiled in water yield a scum like beeswax, capable of being made into aromatic candles. Clan Badge of certain sets of the Campbells.

# 11. Bracken

*(Pteridium Aquilinum)*
*(Gael. Bun Rainnich – Roots)*

**1. Yellowish Green**
Take 2lbs Bracken fronds to 1lb wool
*Method* The best dye comes from the young fronds before they uncurl. Put them in cold water with the wet Alum and Cream of Tartar mordanted wool. Simmer ¾ hour or longer stirring occasionally. Take out the wool. Cool, rinse and dry.

**2. Warm Lime Green**
*Method* As recipe No. 1 but use Chrome mordanted wool and remember to put on a lid.

## BRACKEN ROOTS

**3. Yellow**
*Method* A Portree recipe. No proportions of roots to wool given. Boil the roots for two hours. Strain the liquid into the dyebath. Cool and add Chrome mordanted wool. Cover the dyebath and simmer ½ hour, stirring occasionally. Take out the wool. Cool, rinse and dry.

*Other uses*
Clan Badge of the Robertsons. In October, the bracken or fern on the hill pastures becomes red with the first frosty nights, and about that time the autumnal herbage is very rich; hence, "RED BRACKEN brings milk and butter."

Annabel —

Many thanks - it
is a very useful book but
life is too short to try
them all!

Have a good summer

Madeleine

# 12. Bramble

*(Rubus Fruiticosis)*
*(Gael. Smeuran, an Druise Beannaichte)*

**There are several varieties growing at different altitudes and it is believed all give dye from their berries.**

1. Rose Pink
Use 2lbs berries to 1lb wool
*Method* Using Rubus Fruiticosis, the common variety. Put the ripe berries in a mesh bag or old tights and the wet Alum and Cream of Tartar mordanted wool into the dyebath and cover both with cold water. Bring up to simmer slowly, and simmer and stir occasionally for one hour. Put in hot salt water rinse. Take out the wool, cool, rinse and dry.

2. Green
*Method* Follow the method as in recipe No. 1 but when you take out the wool from the dyebath with a wooden spoon, dip it briefly in a hot solution of 10 – 30% Ammonia (Scrubb's Ammonia is about 10%). Cool, rinse and dry.

3. Purple
*Method* Using the ripe berries in a mesh bag or old tights as in recipe No. 1 but take out the wool and berries after one hour. Dissolve a little Cream of Tartar in the dyebath and then dissolve a little Iron with boiling water in a cup and add to the dyebath. Stir well and put back the wool. Simmer 20 minutes stirring occasionally. Take out the wool and put in hot salt water rinse. Cool, rinse and dry. An iron pot could be used in this recipe in which case you leave out the Iron.

4. Grey/Blue
*Method* Take fresh young shoots of the Bramble and add equal quantities of wool ready mordanted with Alum and Cream of Tartar and cover with cold water. Simmer for one hour stirring occasionally. Lift out the wool, cool, rinse and dry. (For a darker grey, dissolve a little Cream of Tartar in

the dyebath and then dissolve a little Iron in a cup of boiling water before adding it to the dyebath, or use an iron pot.)

Other colours reported:

## 5. Red

John Telfer Dunbar, in the "History of Highland Dress", says they found they got red "using the grain of a kind of Bramble". This would probably be THE STONE BRAMBLE (Rubus Saxatilis) (Gael. Caora Bad Miann). This is found growing in damp rocky thickets throughout the Highland area and climbs to higher elevations than the common Bramble. It has creeping root stock, short stems, small flowers and large red drupelets. The Atlas of British Flora shows it grows on Mull, a lot on Skye and also on hills south of Inverness.

## 6. Orange

There are two recipes from "The Romantic Story of the Highland Garb and the Tartan", but they only give vague directions to boil the wool and Bramble bush together till colour develops. In the Scottish Home Industries Report, Provost Ross also says that orange was obtained from the Bramble. Geoffrey Grigson in "The Englishman's Flora" mentions folklore in the Highlands and says that the root of the Bramble gives an orange dye.

*Other uses*
It is said in Scotland that Christ used this prickly plant to scourge money-lenders in the temple, hence the Gaelic name 'an Druise Beannaichte', 'the Blessed Bramble'.
Clan Badge of the Mac Nab (The Stone Bramble).
Makes excellent jelly preserve.
The leaves were used to place on burns and swellings by 16th century herbalists.

34

# 13. Broom

*(Sarothamnus Scoparius)*
*(Gael. Bealaidh)*

**1. Yellow**
1lb Broom to 1lb wool
*Method* It is best collected when flowering. Cut the flowering tips and put them in the dyebath with wool mordanted with Alum and Cream of Tartar. Cover with cold water and bring up to simmer slowly. Simmer 40 minutes stirring occasionally. Take out the wool, cool, rinse and dry.

**2. Deep Yellow**
*Method* As for recipe No. 1 but use wool mordanted with Chrome and remember to cover with a lid.

**3. Green**
*Method* A Portree recipe. Boil the chopped flowering branches for two to three hours. Strain the liquid into the dyebath. Cool. Insert the wet wool mordanted with Chrome, cover and simmer ½ – one hour, stirring occasionally. Take out the wool, cool, rinse and dry.

In Scotland, Broom has long been used 'over' indigo for a good green, ie – first dye with indigo and then dye with Broom. Known as overdyeing.

*Other uses*
Clan Badge of Forbes and McKay.
Makes good wine and can be eaten in salads.

# 14. Buttercup

*(Ranunculus Flammula)*
*(Gael. Buidheag)*

**Here is an experiment. The following recipe comes from Loch Boisdale where large quantities of the Lesser Spearwort, a member of the Buttercup family grows and flowers in June. I think therefore that Lesser Spearwort is the plant to try.**

1. Purple
*Method* No quantities given. Boil tips of plants with wool till desired colour, then add Baking Soda. (As there is no mordant mentioned, Alum could be tried).

# 15. Cloudberry

*(Rubus Chamaemorus)*
*(Gael. Lus-nan-Eighreag)*

**John Telfer Dunbar in the "History of Highland Dress" says that purple was reported to have been obtained. This creeping rhizome grows on mountains in peat bogs and on the hills on the road to Ullapool and in the Bonar Bridge area. I have not experimented, but suggest the berries should be used as in recipe No. 1 of Blaeberries.**

*Other uses*
The berries are used as a dessert.

# 16. Coltsfoot

**A native perennial of hard, bare places and shingle, it flowers March to April, the flowers appearing before the leaves.**

1. Green Yellow
Take equal quantities of leaves to the weight of wool.
*Method* Put the plant material in the dyebath with wetted Alum and Cream of Tartar mordanted wool. Cover with cold water and bring slowly to simmering point. Simmer ½ hour stirring occasionally. Lift out the wool with a wooden spoon. Cool, rinse and dry.

2. Green Yellow
*Method* As for recipe No. 1 but take out the wool after simmering ½ hour. Dissolve a little Cream of Tartar in the dyebath and then dissolve a little Iron in boiling water in a cup and add to the dyebath. Stir well. Put back the wool and simmer another 20 minutes, stir occasionally. Take out the wool with a wooden spoon. Cool, rinse well and dry.

*Other uses*
In tinder-box days the down was transformed into tinder. The leaves smoked in the manner of tobacco, or a syrup or decoction of them and the flowers, stand recommended for coughs and other disorders of the breast and lungs. Practice, however, seems almost to have rejected it in 1777.

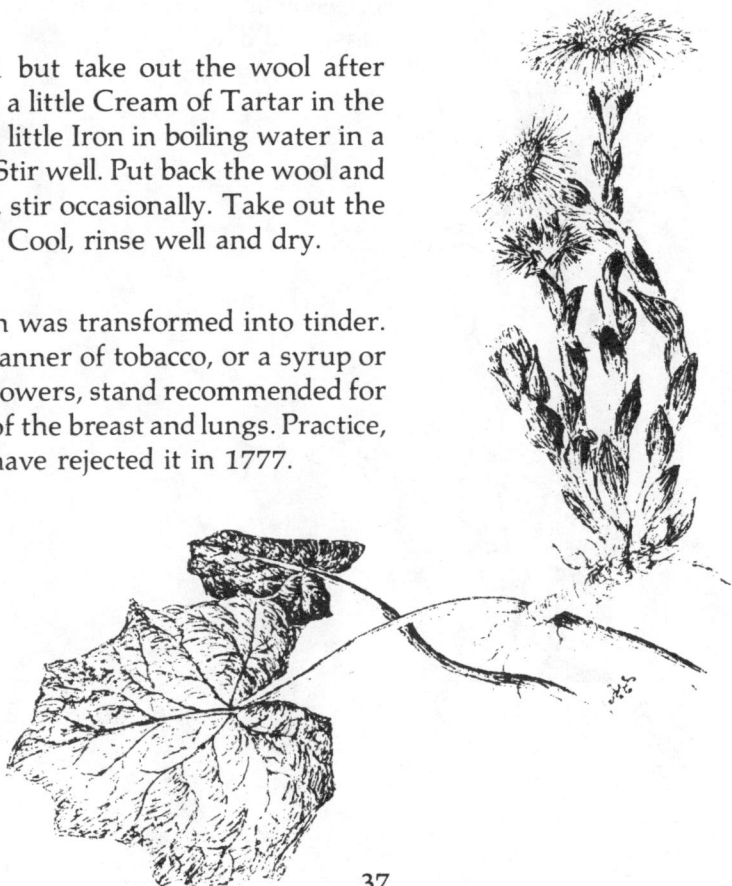

# 17. Corn Marigold

*(Chrysanthemum Segetum)*
*(Gael. Dithean-oir or Neoinean)*

**Fairly common growing as a weed in arable land on the mainland and on the Outer Isles. It flowers between June and August.**

1. Yellow
Take equal weight of flowers to wool.
*Method* This recipe comes from South Uist. Take the flowers and put them in a muslin bag in the dyebath and add the wetted Alum mordanted wool. Cover with cold water. Bring up to simmer slowly and simmer ½ hour, stirring occasionally. Take out the wool with a wooden spoon, cool, rinse and dry.

# 18. Cow Parsley

*(Anthriscus Sylvestris)*

**Prolific throughout the British Isles on roadsides, banks and paths. Flowers April to June.**

1. Yellowish Green
Use twice the weight of plant material to wool.
*Method* Pick the plant when very young and use the flowering tips when in bud also with a few leaves. Put in the wetted wool mordanted with Alum and Cream of Tartar. Cover with cold water and bring slowly to simmering point. Simmer ½ hour stirring occasionally. Take out the wool with a wooden spoon. Cool, rinse and dry.

2. Green
*Method* As for recipe No. 1 but after simmering ½ hour take out the wool and dye material and add a little Copper Sulphate and stir well to dissolve it. When dissolved add the wool and simmer for a further 20 minutes, stirring occasionally. Take out the wool with a wooden spoon and cool, rinse and dry.

*Other uses*
Cow Parsley was connected with the Devil, many of its names are applied as well to the ultra poisonous Hemlock 'Devil's Meal' in Scotland. Used in the making of dyes for Harris Tweed.

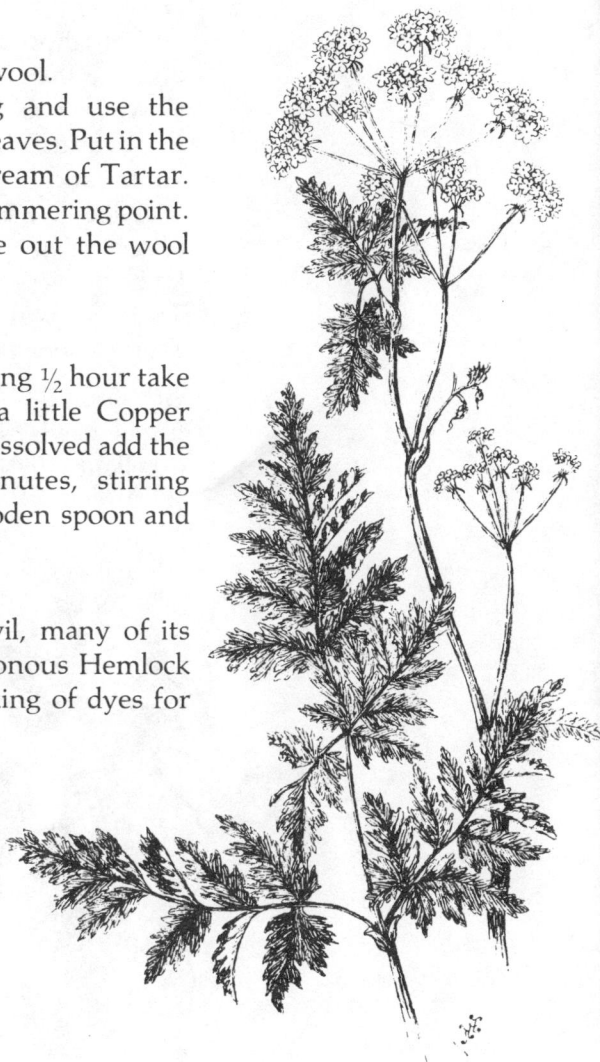

# 19. Crab Apple

*(Pyrus Malus)*
*(Gael. Ubhal-Fiadhaich)*

1. Yellow
1lb bark to ½lb wool (bark taken from fallen trees when possible)
*Method* Chop up and soak the bark in cold water overnight and use the same water for dyeing next morning. Bring it slowly to boil and boil for two hours. Pour off the liquid into the dyebath. Cool and insert wetted wool mordanted with Alum and Cream of Tartar. Simmer ½ hour stirring occasionally. Take out the wool with a wooden spoon, cool, rinse and dry. If a darker shade is required, simmer for longer.
This dye was mentioned as having been used in dyeing Harris Tweed and also at Portree Tweed Mill.

*Other uses*
Juices used for rubbing on sprains, cramps, etc. Makes excellent jelly preserve.

# 20. Crottle

In Scotland, Crottle is the general term for dye lichens and they are differentiated by being called black, dark, white or light Crottle. These Crottles give a wide range of colours. Parmelia Saxatalis and Parmelia Omphalodes are the best known and give a rich wonderful orange brown, while others with fermentation, provide purple, pinks, blue, yellow and green. The Crottles are substantive dyes and require no mordant. When growing on stones they, on the whole, give a better colour than the same ones growing on trees.

It cannot be said too often that the collection of plant material for dyeing should be done with the greatest care and this applies particularly to Crottle growing on rocks, some of which take a lifetime to grow only one inch. Pollution from towns is destroying them so they are something really to be treasured and only small quantities picked.

There are over 40 kinds of Crottle which give a dye, and the Oxford Book of Flowerless Plants is an excellent reference book to help identify different species. Beginners in dyeing need only learn to identify a very few. For instance:

## A. Parmelia Saxatalis
### (Gael. Crotal)

"Staney raw, Stane raw, Scrottyie (Shetland)"
This Crottle is common and grows on trees, walls and rocks except at high altitudes where it is replaced by Parmelia Omphalodes. Gather on windless days when it is wet in late Summer or early Autumn. Scrape off with an old spoon. (It will keep indefinitely when dry.)

1.  Orange Brown
1lb dry Crottle to 1lb dry wool
*Method* Recipe from Loch Boisdale. "Wet the wool and line a vessel with Crottle then ply in layers of wool and Crottle,

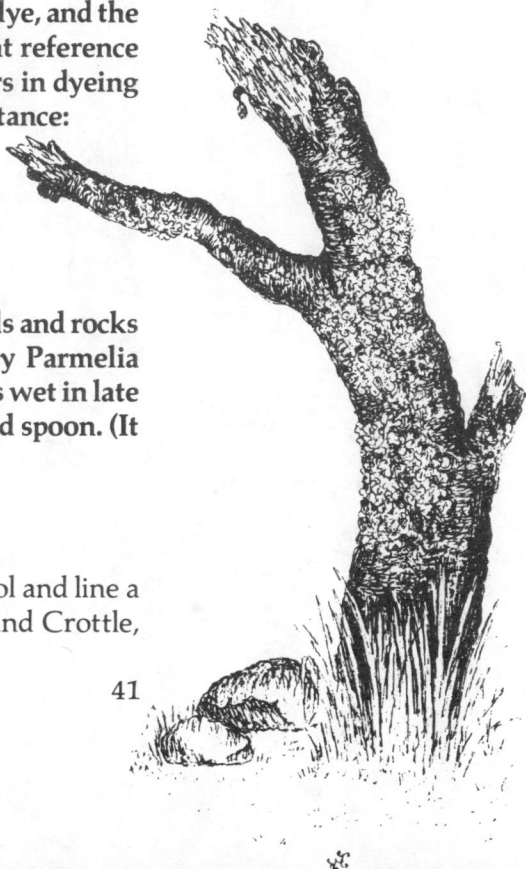

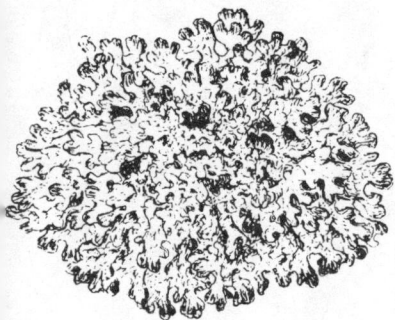

topping it off with Crottle. Fill the pot with cold water until all is covered. Boil on a peat fire if possible, as it gives a slow steady heat; until required depth of colour is seen on wool under the top layer of Crottle, (up to six hours). Remove the pot from the fire and stand it outside for 24 hours to cool. Drain off the water and shake the wool so that the wet Crottle drops out, and lay it out on rocks to dry." Some other recipes say rinse in salt water. Several rinses are advisable to get the wool clean.

"Better the rough stone that yields something than the smooth stone that yields nothing."

## B. *Parmelia Omphalodes*

*(Black Crottle)*
*(Gael. Crotal Dubh)*

**This Crottle grows rather loosely attached to rocks in mountainous districts. Generally collected, if possible on a windless day, in August or September after heavy rain when it comes away more easily.**

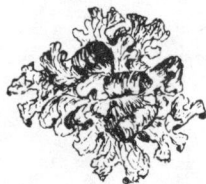

1.   Dark Orange Brown
You will get the most magnificent of the brown dyes, a deep rusty colour startling in its vivacity and it is very fast.
*Method* Recipe from Skye. "Put ply about (put in layers) of Crottle and wool in cold water, bring to boil and simmer for two hours. Pour off the water and dry the material, when the exhausted dyestuff may be shaken out of the wool. (An open or loosely woven bag may be used more than once to exhaust it)." Some recipes say rinse in salt water. Old stockings or tights may be used instead of "a loosely woven bag". If no bag is used several rinses will be needed to get the wool clean.
In "Folksongs and Folklore of South Uist" M. F. Shaw says that Black Crottle can be combined with Cudbear Dye to get a very beautiful red-brown.

# C. Cudbear Dye

*(Ochrelechia Tartarea)*
*(Gael. Corcur, Korkir, Korkalett-Shetland)*
*(White Crottle, Orchil in England)*

**In Scotland this Crottle was fermented with stale urine to obtain a crimson and purple dye but today this process is just as satisfactorily done with Ammonia instead of urine. It grows in roundish patches and is very friable and easily detached from the rocks it is growing on. To help identify this Lichen one may use a dab of household bleach which will turn the Crottle red where it is found. Source for further information on Cudbear Dye see "A Short History of the Orchil Dyes" by Annette Kok.**

Cudbear is produced by fermenting the Crottle with Ammonia, water and oxygen in a warm atmosphere. The temperature needs to be between 56 – 75°Fahr throughout the fermentation period, which varies from 28 days to three weeks. The addition of chalk or lime towards the end of the fermentation period is necessary to give consistency to the mass before making it up into balls. This was done for storage convenience. In the Highlands these balls were wrapped in dock leaves and hung up in peat smoke, being powdered when needed and boiled up with a little Alum. This will keep indefinitely and is always of a dark bluish colour. However, recipes in this book use the dye before the addition of chalk or lime.

## 1. Purple
*Method* Sieve the Crottle to get rid of grit and shale. Empty the powdered Crottle into a wide necked screwtop jar, (an instant coffee jar is suitable), making sure you have a well fitting lid. Moisten the Crottle thoroughly by adding an Ammonia solution made up of one part household Ammonia to two parts water. The whole mixture should just be stirrable. Now put it in a warm place like an airing cupboard or at the back of a stove. From then on until the colour begins to run the mass must be stirred two or three times a day. This will probably happen in about three days. The mixture should smell rather pungent and if it has

slackened, add a little more solution of Ammonia. Once the colour begins to run the mixture needs only to be stirred once a day. The dye may be used when the fermentation has made the colour run full and strong. The time it takes varies but may be between ten days to three weeks. It may be kept stored in a screwtop jar for some weeks.

One tablespoon of the mixture will dye 2oz wool.

Put the wet unmordanted wool in the dyebath with enough water to cover the Cudbear mixture. Simmer for about ½ hour, stirring occasionally. Lift out the wool with a wooden spoon. Cool, rinse and dry.

### 2.  Red

*Method* As described in recipe No. 1 but add a tablespoon of Vinegar to the water before starting to dye.

A note in the "Romantic Story of the Highland Garb and the Tartan" says that Crottle growing on Limestone gives scarlet.

### 3.  Violet

*Method* ½lb wool to 2oz Cudbear powder and one tablespoon washing soda. Mix 2oz Cudbear with one pint of warm water in an enamel container. Stir and mix the water until the powder has completely dissolved and is a thin paste. Put 1½ gallons of warm water in an enamel container and add to it the mixture a little at a time. Heat to simmer for 15 minutes. Stir thoroughly. Add the wet unmordanted yarn to the dyebath and simmer for 20 minutes keeping the temperature below boiling and stir. Dissolve one tablespoon washing soda in half a pint warm water and add this to the dyebath. Simmer it another 20 minutes and stir. Cool and rinse in warm water until the rinse is clear. Hang in the shade to dry.

(Powdered Cudbear Dye can be obtained from dye manufacturers or this recipe could be adapted to use macerated dye solution with Ammonia).

## D. *Evernia Prunastri*

*(Blackthorn Moss)*
*(Other names – Oak Moss, Mousse de Chene)*

Fill a screwtop jar with this Crottle and treat in the same way as for fermenting Cudbear. The Crottle is best dry and should be broken up before use.

1.   Pink
*Method* After one month fermentation, a good pink will be obtained using the dye solution as with the Cudbear recipe No. 1.

2.   Green
*Method* After ten days fermentation, a pale green will be obtained using the solution as above.

3.   Yellow
Take equal quantities of Crottle and wool.
*Method* Simply put the Crottle and wet unmordanted wool in the dyebath and cover with cold water. Bring up to simmering point slowly and simmer about ½ hour, stir occasionally. Take out the wool with a wooden spoon. Cool, rinse and dry.

## E. *Lobaria Pulmonaria*

*(Lung Wort)*

**Only small quantities of this should be used as it takes many years to grow. It grows in western districts.**

1.   Chestnut Brown
Take equal quantities of Lung Wort to Wool.
*Method* Put the Lung Wort and wet unmordanted wool in the dyebath with enough cold water to cover it. Simmer gently for about ¾ hour to get a beautiful rich brown, stirring occasionally. Take out the wool, cool, rinse and dry.

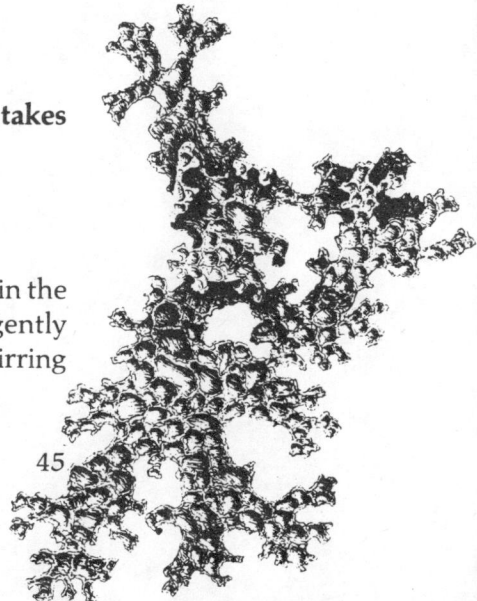

45

# F. (Xanthoria Parientina)

*(Variety Ectanea)*

**This Crottle is known to have been used in South Uist where a rosy pink was obtained.**

1. Rosy Pink
Take equal quantities of Xanthoria Parientina to wool.
*Method* Put the Crottle in the dyebath with wet Chrome mordanted wool and cover with cold water, remembering to put a lid on. Bring slowly to simmering point. Simmer for ¾ hour stirring occasionally. Take out the wool with a wooden spoon and cool. Rinse and dry in the shade.

The following method and use of alterants will give a spectacular range of colours and is a useful way of experimenting with ½oz skeins.
First the Crottle must be put in a large screwtop jar and covered with Ammonia and water solution and fermented in just the same way as for Cudbear, keeping the fermentation going for at least one month. It is best left in a warm place for several months.

2. Blue
Three tablespoons dye solution to ½oz wool.
*Method* Choose a bright sunny day. Using wool mordanted with Alum and Cream of Tartar, put in the dyebath with rain water to cover it and the dye solution. Simmer for 1½ hours, stir occasionally. Take out the wool from the hot dyebath with a wooden spoon and put it into hot soap suds of the same temperature. Rinse in hot rainwater and dry in a towel before spreading it out in full sun, turning often. (It turns blue as it dries).

3. Pink
*Method* As for recipe No. 2 but dry in the shade.

46

### 4. Purple

*Method* As for recipe No. 2 but add Baking Soda to the dyebath and dry in the shade.

*Cautions during the fermentation process*

Slight variations in procedure can produce slight variations in colour or ruin it altogether, ie:

> Warm or cool fermentation place
> Forgetting to stir (no oxygenation)
> Letting it get dried out
> Freezing or leaving in bright sun
> Boiling Crottles before adding Ammonia

*Other uses*

Crottles have a use in the production of Antibiotics and Litmus paper and the oil extracted from Crottle may be used as a fixative for very costly perfumes. Their latest use however is in the detection of pollution as they will not grow in a polluted atmosphere.

*Superstitions*

Parmelia Saxatalis and Parmelia Omphalodes were shunned by fishermen. "Plucked from the rocks return to the rocks." They must always wear something blue if they wear Crottle.

"Crottle reduced to a powder was put on the soles of their hose, as it saved their feet from getting inflamed with the heat when travelling far". It was used in the making of Harris Tweed and it is the plant which gives the "Harris Tweed" smell.

# 21. Crowberry

*(Empetrum Nigrum)*
*(Gael. Dearcan Feannaig)*

**Common on moors and mountains.**

1.   Purple.
1lb ripe berries to 1lb wool.
*Method* Crush the berries in the dyebath and add some soft water to cover – rain water would do. Enter the wetted Alum and Cream of Tartar mordanted wool and push it down among the berries with a wooden spoon. Simmer slowly for one hour stirring occasionally. Lift out the wool. Cool, rinse and dry.

# 22. Currant – Red

*(Ribes Slyvestre)*
*(Gael. Dearcan Dearga)*

**This may be native or introduced. Probably native by
streams and in woods etc, but birds guzzle the berries of the
garden and drop them in hedges where you sometimes find
Ribes Sylvestre for mile upon mile.**

1.   Brown
Equal weight of twigs to wool.
*Method* Boil the twigs for two hours and then strain off the
liquid into the dyebath. Cool. Add the wet wool mordanted
with Alum and Cream of Tartar. Simmer for ½ hour,
stirring occasionally. Lift out the wool with a wooden spoon.
Cool, rinse and dry.

# 23. Dandelion

*(Taraxacum Officinale)*
*(Gael. Bearnan Bride)*

## 1. Magenta

No recipes available, but there are several mentions of the colour magenta having been obtained. Most dyers, including the present writer, obtain only dull yellow-brown. Elsie Davenport in "Your Yarn Dyeing" says, "one specimen gathered by a student of Goldsmith's College, London, from the Dunoon area, undoubtedly produced a purplish red with Alum. It is regarded by botanists as a variable and still evolving genus."

*Other uses*

It is a diuretic in medicine.

Young leaves when blanched used for salad.

"They are recommended thus to be taken for the jaundice and cachexy and in strong decoction for the gravel."

# 24. Devil's Bit Scabious

*(Succisa Pratensis)*
*(Gael. Ura Bhallach)*

**Flowers July to October on heaths and pastures.**

1.   Greenish Yellow
Use 1lb leaves to 1lb wool
*Method* Pick the young fresh leaves and put them in the dyebath with the wet wool mordanted with Alum and Cream of Tartar, cover with cold water and simmer, stirring occasionally, until required shade is reached. Take out the wool. Cool, rinse and dry. It has been stated that leaves prepared and used as woad give blue (Ethel Mairet).

According to an old superstition, the Devil, envying the benefits this plant might confer on mankind, bit away a part of the root – hence the name.

# 25. Dock

*(Rumex Obtusifolius)*
*(Gael. Copag)*

1. Black
1lb roots to 1lb wool
*Method* Recipes using the roots from Loch Boisdale and Portree: Wash the roots well and cut them up. Boil them for two hours. Strain off the liquid into the dyebath. Add a little Chrome and stir and then add the wet wool (remembering to put on the lid). Simmer for ½ hour. Lift out the wool. Cool, rinse and dry. Some other recipes use Iron instead of Chrome.

2. Yellow
1lb leaves to 1lb wool
*Method* Pick the leaves when young and cover with cold water. Boil for two hours. Strain off the liquid into the dyebath. Cool. Add the wetted wool mordanted with Alum and Cream of Tartar. Simmer for one hour stirring occasionally. Lift out the wool with a wooden spoon. Cool, rinse and dry.

3. Warm Brown
*Method* As for yellow but at the end of the hour's simmering, lift out the wool with a wooden spoon and add a little Copper Sulphate. Stir well to dissolve it. Cool. Add the wool and simmer for a further 20 minutes. Lift out the wool, cool, rinse well and dry.

52

# 26. Dog Rose

*(Rosa Canina)*
*(Gael. Muca-faileag-berries)*

**Doctor Maclagan's report on Highland Dyeing says that Briar root and Copperas (Iron) gave black, but no quantities are given.**

*Other uses*
The pulp of the fruit separated from the seeds and mixed with wine and sugar, makes a jelly much esteemed in some countries. The white rose became the emblem of the House of Stuart. The 10th June is White Rose Day when Jacobites wore a white rose. It was the birthday of Prince Charlie. Many of the fine Jacobite glasses had a rose or rose and buds engraved on them.

# 27. Dulse

*(Rhodymenia Palamata)*
*(Gael. Duileasg)*

**SEA WEED The spring tides are the time to collect it on the west coast of Scotland.**

1.   Brown
2lbs Dulse to 1lb wool
*Method* A Portree recipe.
   (a)   Boil the Dulse for two hours. Strain off the liquid into the dyebath. Cool. Add the wetted Alum mordanted wool and simmer stirring occasionally for one hour. Lift out the wool with a wooden spoon. Cool, rinse and dry.
   (b)   This recipe was obtained from an experienced dyer in Mull in 1898:

"Soak the cloth or yarn to be dyed in Alum water and then having prepared a strong infusion of Dulse, sufficient in quantity to cover the material, put the Alum soaked yarn into the infusion while still warm, and keep it moderately warm for four to five days. The continuous heat is found by experience to be only applicable with burning peat."

*Other uses*
In Skye a cure for gravel was taking a broth made with Dulse.
An article in the Celtic Magazine on old Highland remedies says: "Megrin and headache cured by applying the sea plant Linnearach to the side of the head affected and also by a plaster of cold Dulse."

# 28. Elder

*(Sambucus Nigra)*
*(Gael. Droman or Dromanach)*

**DWARF ELDER or DANEWORT can be used in the same way as Elder.**

1(a)   Blue
2lbs Elderberries to 1lb wool
*Method* Crush the berries in the dyebath and cover with cold water. Take the wetted wool mordanted with Alum and Cream of Tartar and push it down among the berries with a wooden spoon. Simmer slowly for $1\frac{1}{2}$ hours stirring occasionally. Lift out the wool with a wooden spoon and put it in a hot salt rinse the same temperature as the dyebath. Lift out the wool, cool, rinse and dry.

1(b)   No quantities given
Simmer the berries with some Elecampane (it grows on the West Coast of Scotland) for about $1\frac{1}{2}$ hours. Then strain off the liquid and cool. Enter the wetted Alum mordanted wool and simmer one hour. Put in salt water, rinse and continue as in 1 (a).

2.   Violet Purple
*Method* As in 1 (a) but use Chrome mordanted wool and remember to use a lid. Rinse in unsalted water.

3.   Yellow
2lbs leaves to 1lb wool
*Method* Chop up the young leaves and put them in the dyebath and cover with cold water. Add the wetted wool mordanted with Alum and Cream of Tartar. Simmer for 30 minutes stirring occasionally. Lift out the wool with a wooden spoon. Cool, rinse and dry. (Alum gives a light yellow, Chrome gives a deep yellow.)

### 4.  Green
*Method* As in No. 3 but lift out the wool after 30 minutes simmering and extract the leaves. Put some Cream of Tartar in the dyebath and dissolve some Iron in a cup with boiling water and stir well in dyebath. Cool to hand heat and then add the wool and simmer for 20 minutes. Lift out the wool with a wooden spoon. Cool, rinse well and dry.

### 5.  Grey
1lb bark to 1lb wool
*Method* Chop up the bark and soak it overnight in the water to be used for dyeing. Simmer for two hours. Strain off the liquid into the dyebath and put in wetted wool mordanted with Alum and Cream of Tartar. Simmer for one to two hours. Take out the wool with a wooden spoon and put some Cream of Tartar in the dyebath and dissolve Iron in a cup with boiling water. Put in the dyebath and stir well then cool to hand heat. Put in the wool and simmer for 20 minutes. Take out the wool. Cool, rinse and dry.

*Other uses*
An old recipe says "Elderberries stewed with Iron, Vinegar and Alum make an excellent ink."
The berries were used in the making of dyes for Harris Tweed. Elder was a guard against witches and fairies. Often an elder tree was planted at the back of the house while the rowan guarded the front.
The bourtree, as the elder is called in Scotland from being so often employed in forming garden bowers, has a bad reputation, as being supposed to have composed the cross on which the Saviour was crucified. Hence a rhyme –

> Bourtree, bourtree, crooked rung,
> Never straight and never strong
> Ever bush and never tree
> Since our Lord was nailed to ye.

# 29. Elecampane

*(Inula Helenium)*
*(Gael. Aillean)*

**Flowers July to August. It grows on Mull, Skye, North and South Uist and Tiree.**

1. Blue
A recipe from the "Romantic Story of the Highland Garb and the Tartan" says that Elecampane, Elder and Salt give blue but no details or quantities are given.

2. Blue
A recipe from "The Gaelic Names of Trees, Shrubs and Plants, 1878" by Charles Fergusson says that "Elecampane gives a very bright blue and was much used. They added some whortleberries to it to improve the colour." Again no details or quantities are given.

3. Blue
In "A Modern Herbal" Mrs. Grieve says a blue dye has been extracted from the roots and bruised and macerated and mingled with ashes and whortleberries. She gives no source of this information.

4. Purple
In "History of Highland Dress 1951" John Telfer Dunbar mentions Elecampane and Whortleberries with Iron and sometimes Verdigris but gives no more details.

*Other uses*
The root was used in herbal cures for asthma and coughs.

# 30. Fir Clubmoss

*(Lycopodiumselago)*
*(Gael. Garbhag-an-t-sleibhe)*

**It usually grows in open, damp places, in clefts between boulders and on rock ledges 250 – 1,750 feet.**

This seems to have been used specifically in place of Alum being used mostly as a base for other colours.
For drying it should be collected in the spring but it can be used fresh all the year round.

1.   Yellow
A recipe from Doctor Maclagan mentions it was used with the foliage of the Blaeberry but no quantities are given. It is also mentioned as being used with St John's Wort and Polyganum Persicaria.

2.   Blue
*Method* From a Portree recipe.
"Boil for two hours with Logwood (imported dye), adding salt. The process of dyeing is to wash the thread thoroughly with liquid Ammonia, then rinse well in cold water, and put into the pot with the dye, which is kept boiling all the time . . . (if Blue, the water is mixed with salt)."

*Other uses*
The Badge of the Campbells
In some parts Fir Clubmoss was used as a dusting powder for the skin.
**Ortha nan Gaidheal –**
> The Clubmoss is on my person
> No harm nor mishap can me befall
> No sprite shall slay me, no arrow shall wound me
> No fay nor dun water-nymph shall tear me.

# 31. Foxglove

*(Digitalis Purpurea)*
*(Gael. Meuran nan Cailleach)*

**Dead Woman's Thimbles, The Fairy Woman's Plant**, (Lus-nan-ban-sith)

A note among some dye recipes at Kingussie Folk Museum mentions Foxgloves and Rowan Berries as having been used together in dyeing, but gave no recipe. An experiment using Alum as a mordant gave no satisfactory result.

# 32. Hawthorn

*(Crataegus monogyna)*
*(Gael. Sgitheach or Preas nan sgeachag)*

1.   Black
*Method* Cut up and soak the bark overnight in the water to be used for dyeing. Boil for two hours. Strain the liquid into the dyebath and cool to hand heat. Put in the wetted wool mordanted with Alum and Cream of Tartar and simmer 20 minutes, stirring occasionally. Lift out the wool and dissolve a little Cream of Tartar in the dyebath and then dissolve some Iron in a cup with boiling water. Put it in the dyebath and stir well. Cool to hand heat, put back the wool and simmer 20 minutes. Lift out the wool with a wooden spoon. Cool, rinse and dry.

2.   Fawn
2lbs berries to 1lb wool
*Method* Put the berries in the dyebath and cover with cold water. Put in wetted wool mordanted with Alum and Cream of Tartar and push it down among the berries with a wooden spoon. Simmer one hour, stirring occasionally. Lift out the wool. Cool, rinse and dry.

*Other uses*
Badge of Ellis and Ogilvy.

# 33. Heather

*(Calluna vulgaris)*
*(Gael. Fraoch)*

**Flowers August to September. The age of the heather makes all the difference to the colour obtained.**

1.   Yellow
1lb flower tips of calluna vulgaris to 1lb wool
*Method* Pick the flower tips just before they open. Put them in to a pan and cover with cold water. Bring up to the boil slowly and boil slowly for two hours. Strain off the liquid in the dyebath. Cool to hand heat. Add wetted wool mordanted with Alum and Cream of Tartar. Simmer for ½ hour stirring occasionally. Take out the wool. Cool, rinse and dry.

2.   Grey Green
*Method* As for recipe No. 1 but at the end of ½ hour simmering, take out the wool, dissolve some Cream of Tartar in the dyebath and also dissolve a little Iron in a cup with boiling water. Add this to the dyebath. Stir and cool to hand heat. Add the wool and simmer 20 minutes. Lift out the wool, cool, rinse well and dry.

3.   Orange
*Method* As for recipe No. 1 but at the end of ½ hour simmering, take out the wool and dissolve a little Cream of Tartar in the dyebath and then dissolve a little Tin in a cup with boiling water. Add this to the dyebath and stir well. Cool to hand heat and add the wool and simmer 15 minutes. Take out the wool and give it a quick wash in hot soapy water. Cool, rinse and dry.

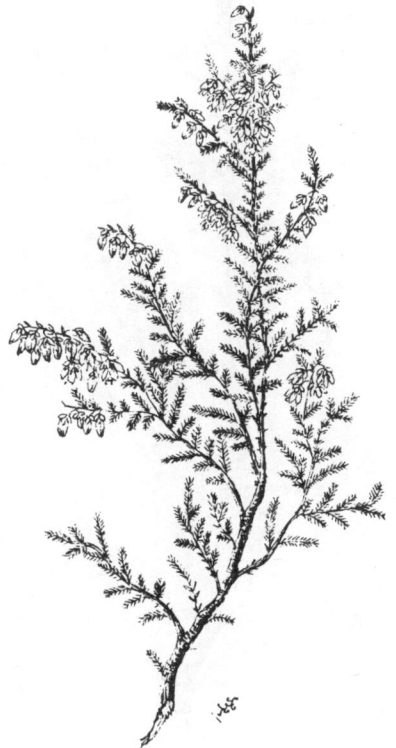

### 4. Brown

*Method* Use the same method as in No. 1 but collect the flower tips when the flowering is over.

### 5. Bronze

*Method* A recipe that gives no details except to use the tips in October with Copper Sulphate.

*Other uses*
It was used in the making of dyes for Harris Tweed.
Clan Badge of the MacDonalds and also their war cry.
Used for thatching (also ropes were made with it in a kind of lattice to keep the thatch on).
Used for tanning on Rhum and Skye making a strong decoction.
For brewing ale in Islay and Jura, 1772, (⅔ of the heather to ⅓ malt).
To make beds by laying the roots downwards, tops upwards.
Rope was made from heather. It was done by two people, one feeding in the heather and the other walking backwards twisting a stick clockwise.

# 34. Bell Heather

*(Erica cinerea)*

## Flowers July to August

Purple
1lb roots to 1lb wool
*Method* Wash, chop and soak the roots in the water to be used for dyeing. Boil for two hours. Strain off the liquid and cool to hand heat. Put in the wetted wool mordanted with Alum and Cream of Tartar and simmer till desired shade, stirring occasionally. Lift out the wool. Cool, rinse and dry.

# 35. Indigo

*(Indigofera tinctoria)*
*(Gael. Quirmean)*

Blue is the colour most difficult to obtain using natural dyes and indigo is the plant material that was imported to produce the colour and used from an early date. In "Highland Shielings in the Olden Times" by Duncan Campbell, it is explained they called it "Quirmean" which is properly the Gaelic name for Woad or "Isatis Tinctoria". Indigo must therefore have taken, long ago, the place of Woad in their list of dyeing materials, but the strange thing is that Woad, which was in so much use for dyeing blue was rare in England by the end of the 1800s and scarcely found in Scotland. In 1410 in an expedition to the Firth of Forth ships laden with woollen and linen cloth, pitch tar, woad and meal were taken as prizes. "Plant" Indigo was imported in lump form and it was thought of as part of a woman's inheritance and treasured. Until after World War I it was still being used in the Outer Isles. It must have been rather a smelly process. Indigo is now produced synthetically.

Here is a selection of old recipes as a record:

*Old recipe from the Outer Hebrides* "Boil wool with onion skins until clear yellow, then let wool dry. Have an old pail filled with urine at least two weeks old, or until skin forms on top. Use wooden tub for dyeing. Put lump indigo in a muslin bag, heat the 'bree' to hand warmth by placing a hot stone in it. Squeeze in the blue bag. Wet the wool and place in the liquid. Cover the wooden vessel and stone where it will keep warm. After 24 hours take the wool out and shake it, do not wring or squeeze. Heat the stone again in the fire and place in 'bree' until hand heat again; replace wool and cover as before. Repeat shaking and reheating every 24 hours for at least seven days. For navy blue, 11 to 21 days are required. Fix with boiled sorrel roots as rinsing water, but do not boil the 'bree' as it loses its properties."

*Recipe from Argyllshire* "Take a six-gallon pot, put into it five gallons of fual (stale human urine), and hang in it a small bag

63

containing indigo. Take the bag out daily and rub it well until the amount of colour required is extracted. In the solution of indigo thus obtained steep the yarn for four or five days, keeping it warm over a slow peat fire, putting in water as required, to compensate the evaporation. The yarn to be left to steep for at least two weeks to obtain a really deep, fast blue."

*Indigo and Sorrel recipe from South Uist* "Save the household urine until sufficient in a big clean tub beside the fire. The temperature must be about 85° to 90° and must not vary. Put the indigo in a little bag of muslin and steep it in the urine. Every three days squeeze it, rubbing it with hands to take the colour out. An ounce of indigo to a pound of wool, but as the strength varies, take what you think will do.

Take Sorrel (Sealbhag – Rumex acetosa), gather the root and stem, wash and clean it but do not break it. Boil this plant, a pound to a pint, until the juice is strong. Strain it and add to the urine. This is the mordant and makes the colour adhere to the wool.
Remove the indigo bag when this is done. Now put the wool in clean hot water, rinse it and put in the urine tub. Put a top on the tub and leave for three days. But every day lift and squeeze the wool and put back again, remembering that the temperature must always be the same."

Dark Green
*Indigo and Sorrel recipe from Howemore, South Uist* (Annie MacIntyre of Howemore, School of Scottish Studies notes) "One large tub urine. Suspend indigo in bag above the tub and dip in tub occasionally and allow to drip. Dip and stir indigo. Cut sorrel small and boil for a day. Now add sorrel juice to tub and boil for one day. Wash wool in hot water and dry well. Put wool in mixture for three to four weeks removing and 'searching' daily. Add sorrel juice to tub every three days. When sufficiently dyed, remove wool and wash well with soap and water."

*A Memory from Mull* (Chrissie MacGillivray, Mull) "We used to have an iron pot outside in the summer time, with just a little heat, not to boil and left it like that for quite a while wringing the wool now and again and putting it back in until the desired shade was reached."

# 36. Iris

*(Pseudacorus)*
*(Gael. Seileasdair or Sealasdair)*

**The roots should be used when the flower is over. There is no record of exact weight of roots used to wool.**

1.   Blue Grey
*Method* A South Uist recipe. "Take the roots when the flower is past. Clean, scrape and cut up then boil in water for two hours. It is then strained and the wool boiled (simmered) with the juice for a good hour or longer, until desired shade of blue or steel grey. A little Alum is used – sometimes the entire plant is boiled with the wool."

2.   Blue Grey
*Method* Another recipe from South Uist from Annie MacIntyre of Howemore, School of Scottish Studies notes. "Wash roots well, crush and boil for a few hours. When the roots are soft, mash up and strain off juice. Put wool in the juice and boil (simmer) for an hour. Add a little Alum and boil for two hours."

3.   Dark Grey
*Method* As above but use Chrome mordant.

4.   Black
*Method* As for 1. or 2. but add some Cream of Tartar and Iron dissolved in a cup with boiling water before you add the wool and simmer for two to three hours to get a real black.

5.   Bright Green
A Kingussie Folklore Museum recipe mentions this colour but gives no details. The leaves and Alum give green.

*Other uses*
Iris was used in the making of Harris Tweed.

# 37. Ivy

*(Hedera Helix)*
*(Gael. E-idheann)*

**The berries are used and are at their best in March or April.**

1.  Greenish Grey
1½lbs berries to 1lb wool
*Method* "Use rather more than an equal weight of berries to the weight of wool and soak for 24 hours. Next day simmer the berries in water for an hour, then allow to cool. Add 1lb wool (previously well washed and still wet) to the dyebath and simmer for about half an hour. Lift out the wool and add the ½oz Iron and 1oz Cream of Tartar which must be dissolved and very well mixed. Then replace the wool. Simmer another half an hour and leave in dyebath until quite cold. Shake off any clinging berries and rinse well and dry."

*Other uses*
The Badge of Gordon.
The berries of Ivy and Privet were used in the making of dyes for Harris Tweed.
In the Highlands and Islands it was thought it kept evil away from the milk, the butter and the animals. An old man in Uist told Alexander Carmichael, author of 'Carmina Gadelica' how he used to swim out to an island in a loch to fetch Ivy, Rowan and Honeysuckle for this protection. Circlets of Ivy alone, or of Ivy plaited with Honeysuckle and Rowan were hung over the lintel of the byre and put under the milk vessels.

# 38. Juniper

*(Juniperis Communis)*
*(Gael. Aiteann)*

1.   Yellow
1lb berries to 1lb wool
*Method* Soak the berries overnight in the water to be used for dyeing. Add the wetted wool mordanted with Alum and Cream of Tartar and simmer for one hour, stirring occasionally. Lift out the wool with a wooden spoon. Cool, rinse and dry.

2.   Brown
The bark also gives a brown dye but no recipe is available.

*Other uses*
Old Highlanders had great faith in Juniper berries as a medicine for almost every disease known amongst them; also for snake bites. In cases of fever or any infectious disease, fires of Juniper bushes were always lighted in or near their houses. They believed that smoke and smell purified the air and carried off all infection.
Juniper berries in hot whisky were taken in moderate doses to treat diarrhoea and dysentry.
Berries were exported from Inverness to Holland for making Dutch Gin.
Clan Badge of the Atholl Highlanders, Gunns, Rosses, McLeods, Murrays and Nicholsons.

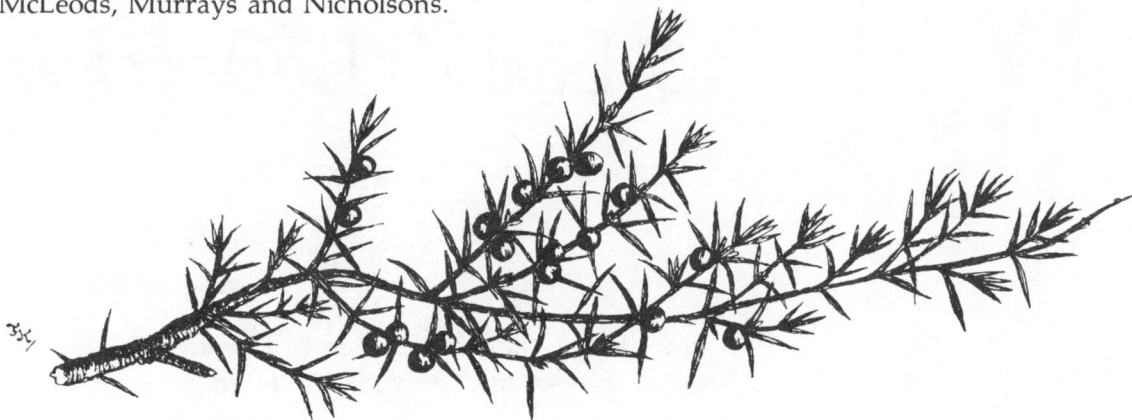

# 39. Knapweed

*(Centaurea Nigra)*
*(Gael. Cnapan Dubh)*

**Flowers June to September.**

1.   Yellow
1lb of the whole young plant to 1lb wool
*Method* Recipe from South Uist. "Boil the whole plant, tops and roots together with the wool using a little Alum, until the colour develops."

2.   Bright Green
*Method* Recipe from Portree. As for No. 1 but use Chrome mordanted wool and keep the dyebath covered.

3.   Green
*Method* As for No. 1 but add Copper Sulphate to the water and dissolve it well and cool before adding the wetted wool.

4.   Rich Dark Brown
*Method* As for No. 1 but after ½ hour lift out the wool and dissolve some Cream of Tartar into the dyebath and stir. Dissolve a little Iron in a cup with boiling water, add to the dyebath and stir, cool to hand heat. Return the wool and simmer 20 minutes. Lift out the wool. Cool, rinse and dry.

# 40. Lady's Bedstraw

*(Galium Verum)*
*(Gael. Ruamh or Bun na Ruamh or Leabadh ban sith)*

**A member of the Madder family Rubiaceae. Found on banks, roadsides and sandy places like the 'machair'.**

1.   Coral Shade
*Method* Recipe from Barra. "First rinse the roots in water to get rid of grit and sand, remove the bark from the roots (this is easily done in very hot water as if one were blanching almonds) as only the bark is used. Put 1oz of Alum into about two quarts of water and bring the solution just to the boil, then add 4oz of root bark and allow to simmer for about 15 minutes. (The best colour is obtained by allowing the decoction to proceed slowly and keeping the dyebath always just below boiling.) The water should now be a strong red colour. Cool, then add the wetted wool (4oz) and simmer again for half an hour or longer. Cool, rinse and wring out the wool."

2.   Crimson
*Method* As in No. 1 but use Chrome mordanted wool and use a lid.

3.   Plum
*Method* As in No. 1 but add some Cream of Tartar to the dyebath and dissolve a little Iron in a cup with boiling water and stir into the dyebath before adding the wool. Or as one recipe says, "put in a handful of copper coins."

4.   Yellow
*Method* Take flowering plants minus the roots and wool of the same weight. Put in the plants into the dyebath and cover with water. Put in the wetted wool mordanted with Alum and Cream of Tartar and push down among the plants with a wooden spoon. Simmer ½ hour, stirring occasionally. Lift out the wool. Cool, rinse and dry.

*Other uses*
The roots were used for a dye in the making of Harris Tweed.
Called "Our Lady's Bedstraw" because, according to a medieval legend, the plant was used during the Nativity. As a reward, its white blossoms were changed to gold.
It was used as a styptic agent.
With nettles and salt, it was used to curdle milk during cheese making, "Lus an leasaich", the rennet plant.

# 41. Madder

*Imported*
*(Rubia Tinctorum)*
*(Gael. Madar Ruadh)*

1.   Fair Isle Red
*Method* A Shetland recipe. "My favourite Fair Isle Red is produced by dyeing rose-coloured Cudbear yarn with Madder. The dyebath is made by boiling 4oz of powdered Madder in a gallon of water for ½ hour. The wool is then simmered in the dye for about the same length of time. The Madder can of course be used alone. (Some people use the Cudbear and Madder together in one operation.)"
Note: Alum has been left out of this recipe by mistake.

*Other information*
Maud or Madder was at one time extensively grown at Aberlady for the use of the Haddington Dyers. The dyers used to dry their yarns on tenters at Tenterfield. (Country Life Section Scottish National Museum).

# 42. Marsh Marigold

*(Caltha Palustria)*
*(Gael. Corrach-shod)*

**KINGCUP Flowers March to July. Found in ditches, wet meadows and shady places.**

1.   Yellow
Equal weight of flowers to wool
*Method* Put the flowers in the dyebath and cover with cold water. Enter the wetted wool mordanted with Alum and Cream of Tartar and push it down with a wooden spoon. Simmer ½ hour stirring occasionally. Lift out the wool and cool. Rinse and dry.

70

# 43. Marsh Woundwort

---

*(Stachys Palustris)*
*(Gael. Lus nan sgor)*

**Grows abundantly in limestone districts, by streams, ponds, ditches and marshes. Flowers July to September.**

1. Yellow
Equal weight of plant to wool.
*Method* (In Shetland the colour is called "Hundie")
Put the whole plant in the dyebath picking them when young. Cover with cold water and insert the wetted wool mordanted with Alum and Cream of Tartar, pushing it down with a wooden spoon. Simmer ¾ hour. Lift out the wool and cool. Rinse and dry.

2. Blue
*Method* 1oz Logwood added to every nine pints water. Marsh Woundwort was said by Mr Edmonston, Balta Sound, Shetland, 1844, to give blue but no mordant was mentioned.

3. Red
He also said "Tormentilla officinalis roots may be used with Marsh Woundwort to give red." Again no mordant was mentioned.

# 44. Meadow Sweet

*(Filipendula Ulmaria)*
*(Gael. Lus-Chuchulainn)*

QUEEN OF THE MEADOW

**Flowers June to August. Found in marshy ground. The plant is ready to use towards the end of May before the flowers open.**

1. Yellow
*Method* Use the flowers, stalks and leaves and cut them up and put them in the dyebath. Cover with cold water and enter wetted wool mordanted with Alum and Cream of Tartar, pushing it down with a wooden spoon. Simmer ¾ hour stirring occasionally. Lift out the wool and cool. Rinse and dry.

2. Green
*Method* As for No. 1 but lift out the wool after simmering ¾ hour and dissolve some Cream of Tartar in the dyebath. Dissolve a little Iron in a cup with boiling water and add to the dyebath. Stir. Cool to hand heat and enter wool for a further 20 minutes simmering. Lift out the wool and cool. Rinse well and dry.

3. Black
*Method* Mr Edmonston, Balta Sound, Shetland, 1844 gives the following recipe: "Sometimes the whole plant was used but more often just the root. Gathered towards the end of May before the flowers expand it was dried in the sun and then boiled slowly for two or three hours in soft water in the proportions of a large handful to three Scotch pints. The water evaporated is replaced by stale urine and the mixture allowed to cool. The cloth which has previously been rubbed

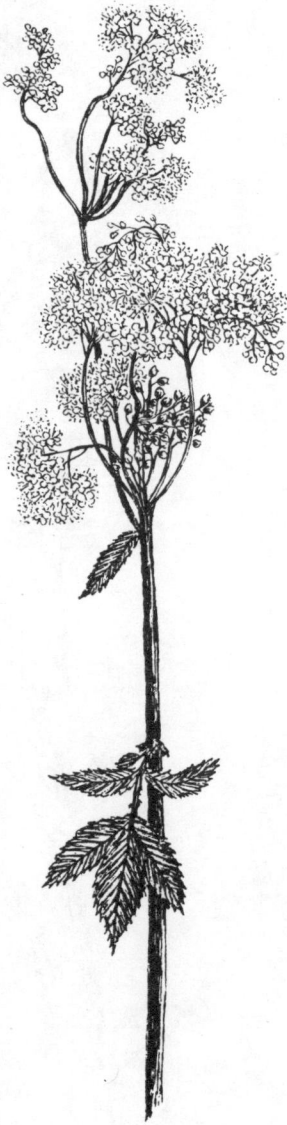

over with bog Iron Ore powdered and moistened with water, is rolled up and boiled in the dye."

4.   Rosy Red
*Method* Elsie Davenport in "Your Yarn Dyeing" says she got a rosy red from the roots with Alum.

*Other uses*
This plant was used in the dyeing of Tartan.
Once used to flavour mead and to cure malaria.
The Gaelic name of Chrios Chu-chulainn is translated, 'The belt of Cu Chulainn' the legendary warrior and hero of Ulster.

# 45. Nettles

*(Urtica)*
*(Gael. Feanntag)*

**Cut the nettles when young using gloves and picking the fresh young green tops.**

1.   Yellow
*Method* Put the nettles in the dyebath and cover with cold water. Enter the wetted wool mordanted with Alum and Cream of Tartar and push it down with a wooden spoon. Simmer slowly for ¾ hour, stirring occasionally. Lift out the wool and cool. Rinse and dry.

2.   Grey Green
*Method* As for recipe No. 1 but after simmering the wool for ¾ hour take it out and dissolve some more Cream of Tartar in the dyebath. Dissolve a little Iron in a cup with boiling water and stir into the dyebath. Cool to hand heat, then enter the wool and simmer a further 20 minutes stirring occasionally. Lift out the wool and cool. Rinse and dry. An iron pot could be used instead of the Iron mordant.

*Other uses*
Nettles were used in the making of dyes for Harris Tweed.

In Arran and other islands a rennet used to be made of a strong decoction of nettles. A spoonful of the liquor would coagulate a large bowl of milk. A quart of salt is put to three pints of the decoction and bottled for use.

A poultice of chopped nettle tops and raw whites of egg applied to the forehead and temples at bedtime was also used to induce sleep. Nettle tops in the spring were often boiled and eaten by the common people instead of cabbage-greens.

> If they wad drink nettles in March
> And eat Muggons in May
> Sae mony braw maidens
> Wadna gang to the clay.

# 46. Oak

*(Quercus)*
*(Gael. Darach)*

**Bark, Acorns and Galls**

1.   Brown
2lbs bark to 1lb wool
*Method* The bark gives a substantive dye if it is boiled for 1½ hours. Then strain off the liquid into the dyebath and cool to hand heat. Enter the wetted wool and simmer for one hour. Cool, rinse and dry.

2.   Black
*Method* Use the bark, acorns and/or galls as in recipe No. 1 and take out the wool after one hour simmering. Dissolve Cream of Tartar in the dyebath and dissolve a little Iron in a cup with boiling water. Stir in the dyebath. Cool to hand heat, enter wool and simmer 20 minutes. Lift out the wool and cool. Rinse and dry.

*Other uses*
Clan Badge of the Kennedys and Moncrieffes.

74

# 47. Onion Skins

**The dry outer skins can often be obtained from greengrocers. A large paper bagful would be needed for 1lb wool.**

1.   Burnt Orange
*Method* Put the onion skins in the dyebath and cover with plenty of cold water. Enter the wetted wool mordanted with Alum and Cream of Tartar and push it down with a wooden spoon. Simmer for one hour, stirring occasionally. Lift out the wool and cool. Rinse and dry.

2.   Brass Colour
*Method* As in recipe No. 1 but use Chrome mordanted wool.

3.   Orange
*Method* As in recipe No. 1 but use a Tin mordant after simmering for one hour. Lift out the wool and dissolve the Tin in a cup with boiling water before stirring it into the dyebath. Cool to hand heat then enter the wool and simmer, stirring occasionally for 20 minutes. Lift out the wool and wash in hot soapy water. Lift out and cool. Rinse and dry.

4.   Moss Green
*Method* As in recipe No. 1 but after simmering for one hour, take out the wool and dissolve some Cream of Tartar in the dyebath and dissolve a little Iron in a cup with boiling water. Add this to the dyebath, stir and cool to hand heat. Add the wool and simmer 20 minutes. Lift out the wool and cool. Rinse well and dry.

*Other uses*
Onion skins were used in the making of dyes for Harris Tweed.

# 48. Peat Soot

1. Auburn Yellow/Brown
*Method* Recipe from South Uist. "Put the soot in a muslin bag, and boil it in water for at least one hour. Lift it and squeeze it and then put the wool in and simmer until required shade."

*Other uses*
Peat soot was used in the making of dyes for Harris Tweed.

Peat Soot.

# 49. Pine Cones and Larch Needles

**The Larch was introduced into Scotland in 1738 and the Fir in 1682.**

## SCOTCH FIR

1.   Light Brown
*Method* Pine cones gave a soft dull light brown, but if picked in early autumn, it was possible to get a reddish yellow dye from them. No mordant or quantities given.

*Other uses*
Clan Badge of the Grants.

## LARCH

2.   Brown
*Method* In autumn the needles of the Larch were used to dye brown. No mordant or quantities given.

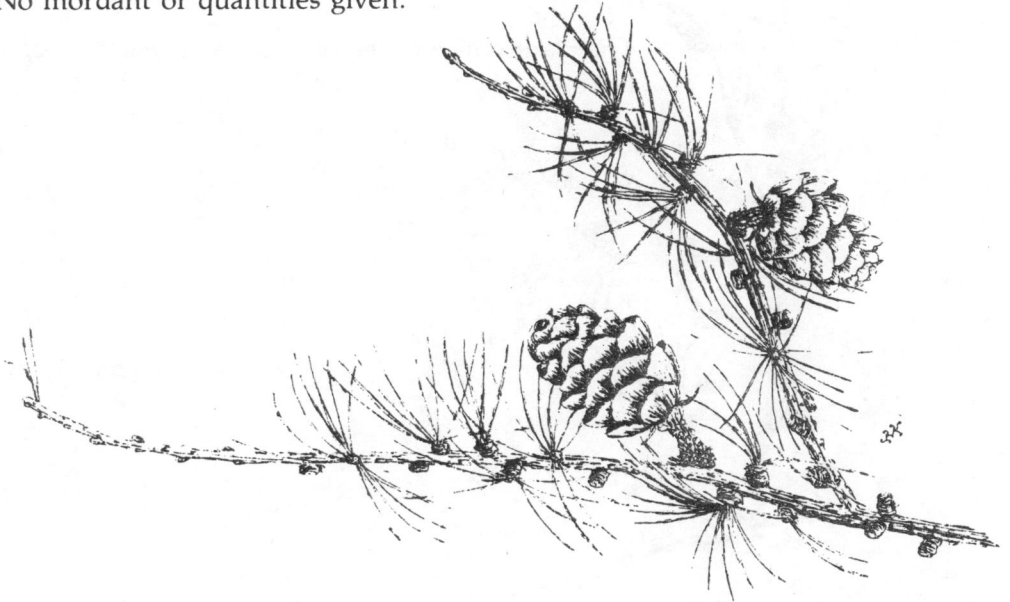

# 50. Polyganum Hydropiper

*(Gael. Lus an Fhogair)*

**SPOTTED KNOTWEED, WATERPEPPER, RED KNEES. It grows in wet places, in streams, ponds and ditches. Distinguished too by the hot peppery taste of the leaves. Flowers July to October.**

1.   Yellow
No quantities given.
*Method* To prepare the dye, soak one peck of the chopped plant for three or four days, then bring to the boil. Simmer for 30 minutes. Strain liquid into dyebath. Enter wetted wool mordanted with Alum and Cream of Tartar and simmer for one hour. Lift out the wool and cool. Rinse and dry.

2.   Gold
*Method* As in recipe No. 1 but use Chrome mordanted wool.

*Other uses*
The plant which expels or banishes. It had the reputation of driving away pain, flies, etc.

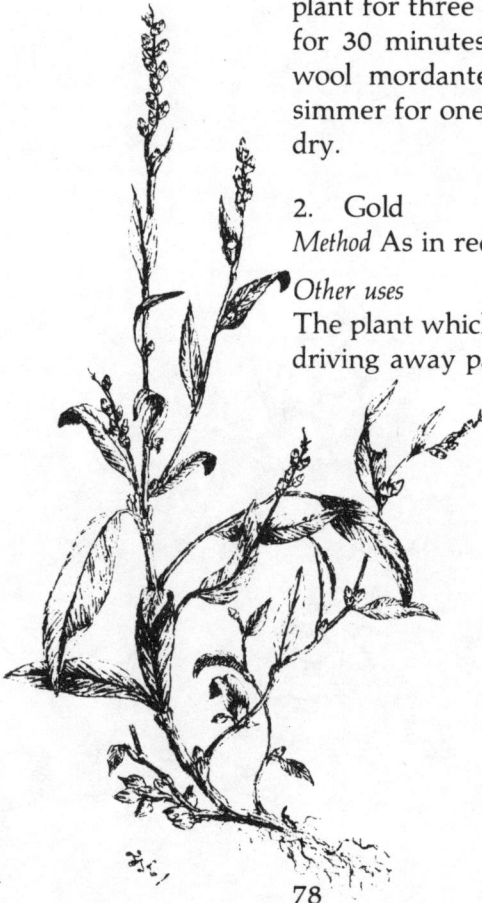

# 51. Polyganum Persicaria

*(Gael. Lus chrann ceusaidh)*

**SPOTTED ARSSMART The herb under the crucifixion tree.**
**Flowers June to September on waste ground by water and as an arable weed. This is easily recognised by the dark spot on its leaves which has been attributed in legend to the plant growing under the Cross and the leaves being spotted by drop after drop of Christ's blood.**

1.   Yellow
*Method* As in recipe No. 1 of Polyganum Hydropiper.

2.   Gold
*Method* As in recipe No. 2 of Polyganum Hydropiper.

*Other information*
The Fir Club Moss is specially mentioned as having been used with Polyganum Persicaria.

# 52. Poplar

*(Populus Tremula)*
*(Gael. Craobh chrithinn, a'chritheann)*

**1.  Yellow**
1lb young leaves to 1lb wool
*Method* Put the leaves in the dyebath, cover with cold water and soak overnight in the water to be used for dyeing. Put in the wetted wool mordanted with Alum and Cream of Tartar and push it down among the leaves using a wooden spoon. Simmer for one hour, stirring occasionally. Lift out the wool and cool. Rinse and dry.

**2.  Gold**
*Method* As in recipe No. 1 but use Chrome mordanted wool.

**3.  Brown**
2lbs bark to 1lb wool
*Method* Chop up and soak the bark overnight. Next day boil bark and water for two hours and strain off the liquid into the dyebath. Cool to hand heat and enter the wetted wool mordanted with Alum and Cream of Tartar. Simmer for one hour stirring occasionally. Lift out the wool and cool. Rinse and dry.

**4.  Black**
*Method* As in recipe No. 2 but after simmering for one hour, dissolve some Cream of Tartar in the dyebath and dissolve a little Iron in a cup with boiling water and add it to the dyebath and stir. Cool to hand heat and enter the wool and simmer for 20 minutes. Lift out the wool and cool. Rinse and dry.

*Other uses*
Clan Badge of the Fergussons.

# 53. Privet

*(Ligustrum vulgare)*
*(Gael. Priobaid)*

1. Greyish Green
1½lbs berries to 1lb wool
*Method* Put the ripe berries into the dyebath and cover with cold water. Enter the wetted wool mordanted with Chrome and push it down among the berries using a wooden spoon. Simmer ¾ hour, stirring occasionally. Lift out the wool and cool. Rinse in salted water and dry.

2. Grey/Blue
A Harris Tweed note mentions berries of Ivy and Privet giving "this grey/blue colour".

# 54. Ragwort

*(Senecia Jacobea)*
*(Gael. Buadhghallan)*

**RAGWEED, STINKING WILLIE The whole plant may be used. It is best picked when it is young. Found on waste ground, roadsides and, as a weed, on grazing land. Flowers June to October.**

1. Bronze
*Method* Cut up the whole plant and put it in the dyebath and cover with cold water. Enter the wetted wool mordanted with Alum and Cream of Tartar and push it down among the plants with a wooden spoon. Simmer about one hour, stirring occasionally. Lift out the wool and cool. Rinse and dry.

2. Yellow

*Method* As in recipe No. 1 but use only the flower heads and simmer ½ hour.

3. Green

*Method* As for recipe No. 1 but lift out the wool after simmering one hour and dissolve some Cream of Tartar in the dyebath. Dissolve a little Iron in a cup with boiling water and stir into the dyebath. Cool to hand heat and enter the wool. Simmer 20 minutes. Lift out the wool and cool. Rinse well and dry.

*Other uses*

Ragwort was a plant used by fairies for locomotion. The fairies of the Highlands and Islands rode sticks of Ragwort across the straits from one island to the next. In Burns' poem the Devil and his hags and his male witches ride together.

> Let Warlocks grim, an' whither'd Hags
> Tell how wi' you on ragweed nags,
> They skim the muirs an' dizzy crags
> Wi' wicked speed.

The Scots are said to have called this plant Stinking Willie after William Duke of Cumberland.

# 55. Reed

*(Phragmites communis)*
*(Gael. Cuilc)*

**Grows in marshes and pools. Flowers August to October.**

1.  Green
1lb flower heads to 1lb wool
*Method* Pick the flower heads when very young and before they open. Put them in the dyebath and cover with cold water and simmer for ½ hour. Cool to hand heat and enter the wetted wool mordanted with Alum and Cream of Tartar. Simmer for another ½ hour. Lift out the wool and cool. Rinse and dry.
For a darker green, add some Iron or use an iron pot.

# 56. Reindeer Moss

*(Cladonia Rangiferina)*

**Grows at 250ft – 1,750ft. This lichen has hollow, much branched fruiting branches, three or four inches high, with a slightly mealy, light grey surface and no permanent horizontal thallus. This is found growing with moss among heather. It is eaten by the deer. No mordant is needed.**

1. Light Brown
1lb moss to 1lb wool
*Method* Cover the moss and wool with cold water and simmer for one hour, stirring occasionally. Take out the wool and cool. Rinse and dry.

2. Dark Red Brown
*Method* As in recipe No. 1 but simmer for two to three hours, stirring occasionally.

3. Dark Brown
*Method* As in recipe No. 2 but leave the dyebath to stand with the wool in it overnight.

# 57. Rowan

*(Sorbus/Aucuparia)*
*(Gael. Caorunn)*

*As an Additive*

The berries can be used to give an extra bright colour when dyeing with Madder and Cochineal.

Rowan berries and Foxglove flowers were reported to give a bright orange dye by the Kingussie Folklore Museum notes. A test using Alum as the mordant was unsuccessful.

*Superstitions*

Rowan trees were believed to guard against witchcraft, hence trees planted often near cottages, and a rod of rowan was used to drive cattle.

*Other uses*

Clan Badge of the Maclachlans and Malcolms.

In some places the berries were distilled to make a very good spirit. The juice was used for an acid punch in Jura and the berries were sometimes eaten when thoroughly ripe.

"It is probable that this tree was in high esteem with the Druids for it may to this day be observed to grow more frequently than any other in the neighbourhood of those Druidical circles of stones, so often seen in North Britain and the superstitions still continue to retain a great veneration for it, which was undoubtedly handed down to them from early antiquity. They believe that any small part of this tree carried about them, will prove a sovereign charm against all the dire effects of enchantment or witchcraft. Their cattle also, as well as themselves, are supposed to be preserved by it from evil; for the dairy-maid will not forget to drive them to the shealings or summer pastures with a rod of the Rowan tree, which she carefully lays up over the door of the sheal, bothy or summer house, and drives them home again with the same. In Strathspey they make, for the same purpose, on the first day of May, a hoop of the wood of this tree, and in the evening and morning cause all the sheep and lambs to pass through it." "Flora Scotica"

# 58. Rue

---

*LESSER MEADOW RUE*
*(Thalictrum minus)*
*(Gael. Ru)*

**A native perennial of dry limestone slopes, cliffs, sand dunes and on damp ground by streams and lochs. Fairly common on northern coasts. Flowers June to August. Lesser Meadow Rue grows in North Uist.**

1.   Red

*Method* Recipe from North Uist. "Use the roots, boil for two hours then boil (simmer) wool in the liquid until the desired colour is obtained." As there is no mention of mordant, Alum and Cream of Tartar is suggested.

# 59. Rush

*(Eleocharis palustris)*
*(Gael. Luachair)*

**Flowers May to July. Grows in land that needs draining.**

1.   Green
1lb Rush flowers to 1lb wool
*Method* Put the pinkish flowers of the Rush in a pan and cover with cold water. Boil slowly for two hours. Strain the liquid into the dyebath and cool to hand heat. Enter the wetted wool mordanted with Alum and Cream of Tartar and simmer ¾ hour, stirring occasionally. Lift out the wool and cool. Rinse and dry.

# 60. St. John's Wort

*(Hypericum perforatum, also Hypericum maculatum)*
*(Gael. Lus na Maighdinn Muire, Achlaisean Chaluim Chille)*

**VIRGIN MARY'S HERB, ARMPIT PACKAGE OF COLUMBA.**

**Hypericum Perforatum is common especially on calcareous soils. Flowers July to September.**

**Hypericum maculatum grows in moist places and is local. Flowers July to September.**

The colour depends on a tiny intensely dark violet gland on the anther which contains a reddish-violet fluid which dyes fingers red if the bud and flowers are crushed with the hand. Although the roots and other parts of the plants may also be used for dyeing, it is mostly the clusters of buds and flowers that are used.

1.   Red
*Method* Put the flower heads in the dyebath and cover with cold water and simmer for one hour. Cool to hand heat and add the wetted wool mordanted with Alum and Cream of Tartar and simmer ½ hour stirring occasionally. Take out the wool and dissolve some Cream of Tartar in the dyebath, then dissolve some Tin in a cup with boiling water before stirring it into the dyebath. Return the wool and simmer 20 minutes. Take out and wash the wool in hot soapy water. Cool, rinse and dry.
A note from another source says the flower buds in vinegar give crimson, but no quantities or mordants are given.

*Other uses*
The plant has been the subject of religious as well as medicinal beliefs since heathen times.
St John's Wort was called the "Milking Plant" as it was put in the pail and then they milked onto it to improve the milk yield. The flowers put in whisky gave it a dark purple tinge almost like port wine.

88

St John's Wort has been used in brewing beer and aquavit.
Ortha nan Gaidheal Volume II:

> "St John's Wort St John's Wort
> My envy whosoever has thee
> I will pluck thee with my right hand
> I will preserve thee with my left hand
> Whoso findeth thee in the cattle fold
> Shall never be without kine."

# 61. Sea Ivory

*(Ramalina Scopulorum)*
*(Gael. Fiasag nan creag)*

**BEARD OF THE ROCK Grows abundantly wherever there are rocks exposed at high-water mark and above. The flattened branches grow in tufts which hang downwards and are pale greenish-grey, smooth and shining. The spore-producing apothecia appear as raised yellowish-grey discs.**

1. Orange Brown
*Method* No mordant required. Pick in May and put in a pan and boil for 1½ hours. Strain off the liquid into the dyebath and cool to hand heat. Enter the wetted wool and simmer ½ hour, stirring occasionally. Lift out the wool and cool. Rinse and dry.

*Other information*
Sea Ivory is known to have been used in Shetland and South Uist for dyeing.

# 62. Sorrel

*(Rumex Acetosa)*
*(Gael. Sealbhag Ruanaidh)*

Found in grassland, roadsides and woods. Flowers May to June. From information given by Mr R. Haggarty of Benbecula, sorrel roots were used as a mordant for most flowers "as a fastner well powdered and boiled to a degree."

1. Red
*Method* "In the winter, use the root and in the summer, the entire plant. Use a little Alum to set the colour. If used alone, it makes red."

2. Ancient Red
*Method* "Sorrel mordant with Tormentil for Ancient Reds." (See Tormentil recipe).

*Other uses*
The leaves may be added to a salad to sharpen the taste. Also nice in a sauce instead of lemon juice.

# 63. Sundew

*(Drosera Rotundifolia)*
*(Gael. Lus na Fearnaich)*

A native perennial of bogs, wet moors and heaths. Flowers June to August. Several sources say that the Sundew gives purple. Dr Maclagan in 1898 says the dried leaves produced a rusty red but not purple. It is said to give purple with Ammonia and Iron.

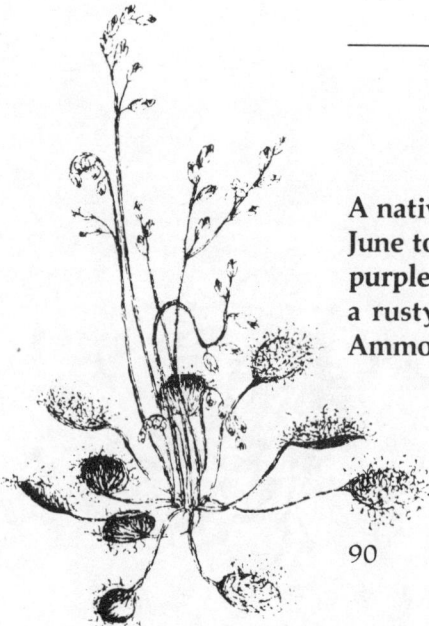

# 64. Tansy

*(Tanacetum vulgare)*
*(Gael. Barr a' Bhrisgein)*

**A native perennial found in hedgerows, roadsides and waste places. Flowers August to September.**

1. Bronze
1lb plant material to 1lb wool
*Method* Use the whole plant and pick it when it is young. Cut up and put it in the dyebath and cover with cold water. Enter the wetted wool mordanted with Alum and Cream of Tartar and push it down among the plants with a wooden spoon. Simmer about one hour, stirring occasionally. Lift out the wool and cool. Rinse and dry.

2. Yellow
*Method* As in recipe No. 1 but only use the flower heads just before they come into flower. Simmer ½ hour.

*Other uses*
The name Tansy is derived from an old name for herb-flavoured omelettes.
Tansy used to be grown in gardens for cooking and many medicinal uses. The roots taste like parsnips and were frequently eaten either boiled or roasted. "In Tyree and Coll they answer the purpose of bread to some measure sometimes have supported the inhabitants for months during scarcity of other provisions."

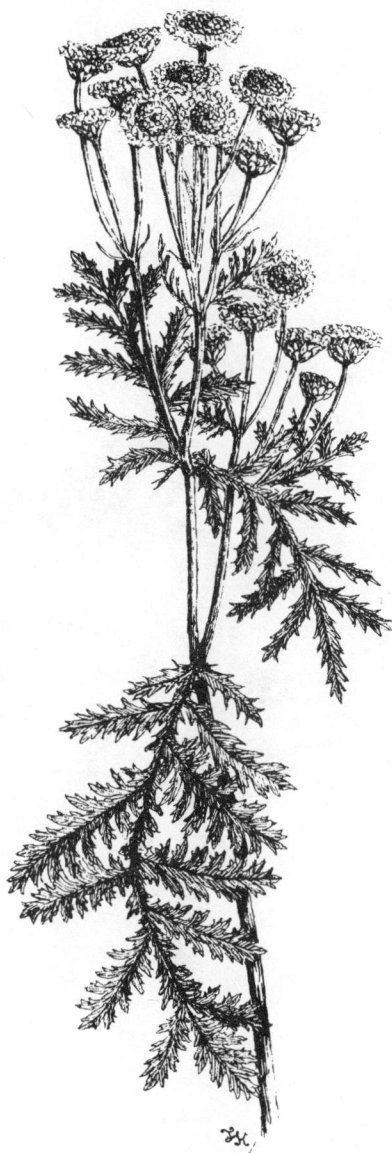

91

# 65. Thistle

*(Cirsium vulgare)*
*(Gael. Cluaran, Foghnan, Diogan, Giogan)*

1.   Emerald Green
1lb plant material to 1lb wool
*Method* Take some yarn that has been dyed with indigo and simmer it slowly with the tips of young thistle plants picked and cut up before coming into flower. Simmer ¾ hour. Lift out the wool and cool. Rinse and dry.

*Other uses*
Clan Badge of the Royal Stuarts.
"The tender leaves strip'd of their spines, are by some boiled and eaten as garden stuff.
An emulsion of the seeds has sometimes been used to thin the blood and to cure stitches and pleurises but at present is rarely practised."

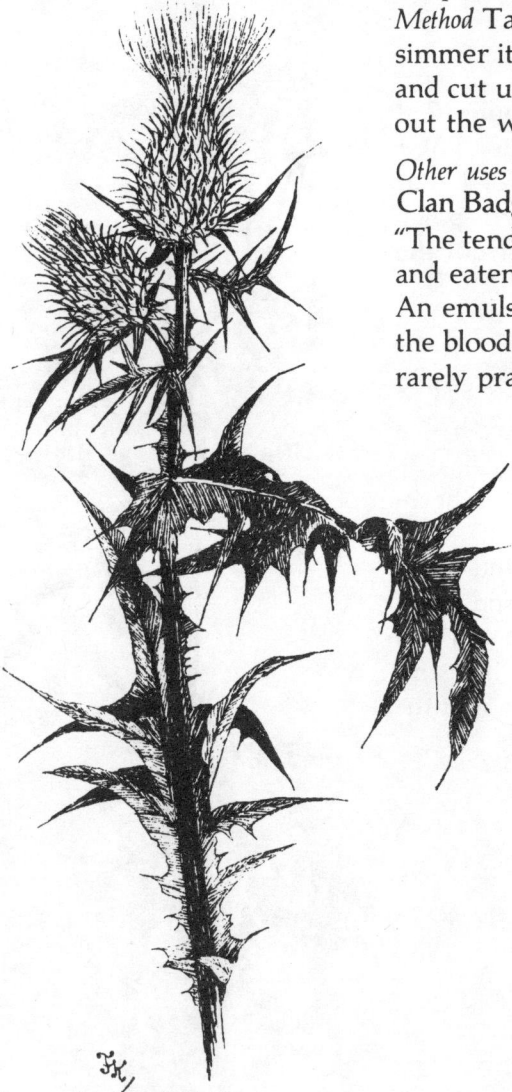

# 66. Tormentil

*(Potentilla Erecta)*
*(Gael. Leannartach)*

**Very common on grassland, mountains, heaths and bogs.**

1.  Red
*Method* Recipe from Benbecula. "Sorrel was used as the mordant for an Ancient Red and the roots of Tormentil were pounded and boiled. The outer skin was scraped off and then boiled."

Miss Elsie Davenport in "Your Yarn Dyeing" says the roots with Alum gave a Rose Red and Purplish Red with Chrome.

*Other uses*
In the Western Isles, the fishermen tanned their nets with Tormentil roots.
In Shetland, it could be used as a substitute for tanner's bark (which was usually Oak).

# 67. Walnut

*(Juglans Regia)*
*(Gael. Craobh – ghallchno)*

1.  Light and Dark Browns
1lb husks to 1lb wool
*Method* Walnut is a substantive dye and needs no mordant.
Put the husks, when black, in the dyebath and cover with
cold water. Enter the wetted wool and push down among
the husks with a wooden spoon. Simmer till you get the
required shade, stirring occasionally. Lift out the wool and
cool. Rinse and dry.

*Other uses*
The Scottish Home Industries record that Walnut root was
used and to collect it before the sap was rising.

# 68. Water Lily

*White*

---

*(Nymphaea alba)*
*(Gael. Cairt-Locha, Gucagan-baite)*

**Water Lilies are prolific in Lismore's strongly alkaline lochs. They are plentiful in North and South Uist, Skye, Harris, Islay and Argyll. A special raft was made to go out on the lochs to gather the roots, which are always in treacherous mud and most difficult to lift. A special hook was used to cut them with.**

1.   Black

*Method* Recipe from South Uist. Scrape and scrub the roots until clean, then beat and pound with a wooden beater till soft. Boil and strain until the liquid is clear. Cool to hand heat and enter the wetted wool mordanted with Alum and Cream of Tartar. Boil till a rich brown. Then lift out the wool and dissolve Cream of Tartar in the dyebath and dissolve a little Iron in a cup of boiling water. Stir in the dyebath and put back the wool. Simmer till you get a fine black.

Miss I F Grant in "Highland Folk Ways" mentions a Fugitive Blue obtained from Water Lily roots, and Kingussie Folklore Museum notes mention Water Lily and Flag Iris root and Alum together.

# 69. Weld

*(Reseda Luteola)*
*(Gael. Lus Buidhe Mor)*

## DYER'S ROCKET, DYER'S GREENWEED

**Cáre must be taken to pick the plant while still young and before it goes to seed. Quite rare in Scotland. Found on chalky soils, waste places, ploughed fields and disturbed ground. Flowers May to August.**

1. Lemon Yellow
*Method* Chop up the whole plant except the roots and boil for two to three hours. Strain off the liquid into the dyebath and cool to hand heat. Enter the wetted wool mordanted with Alum and Cream of Tartar. Simmer ½ hour. Lift out the wool and cool. Rinse and dry.

2. Golden Yellow
*Method* As for recipe No. 1 but enter wetted wool mordanted with Chrome and simmer ½ hour, stirring occasionally. Lift out the wool and cool. Rinse and dry.

3. Orange Yellow
*Method* As for recipe No. 1 but lift out the wool after ½ hour simmering, dissolve some Cream of Tartar in the dyebath and dissolve a little Tin in a cup with boiling water. Stir and enter the wool and simmer 20 minutes. Lift out the wool and wash in soapy hot water. Cool, rinse and dry.

4. Olive Green
*Method* As for recipe No. 1 but after ½ hour simmering, lift out the wool and dissolve some Cream of Tartar in the dyebath. Dissolve a little Iron in a cup with boiling water and stir into the dyebath. Cool to hand heat and enter the wool and simmer 20 minutes, stirring occasionally. Lift out the wool and cool. Rinse well and dry.

*Other uses*
Weld is mentioned as having been used in the making of Harris Tweed.

96

# 70. Whin

*(Ulex Europeaus)*
*(Gael. Conas)*

**GORSE**

1.   Yellow
1lb flowers to 1lb wool
*Method* Put the flowers in the dyebath and cover with cold water. Enter the wetted wool mordanted with Alum and Cream of Tartar. Simmer ¾ hour, stirring occasionally. Lift out the wool and cool. Rinse and dry.

2.   Old Gold
*Method* Use the flowers as in recipe No. 1 but with Chrome mordanted wool and remember to put on the lid.

3.   Green
1lb bark and some young foliage to 1lb wool.
This must be picked in April or May.
*Method* Chop up the bark and soak it overnight in the water to be used for dyeing. Boil for two hours and strain off the liquid into the dyebath and cool. Enter the wetted wool mordanted with Chrome. Put on the lid and simmer for ½ hour stirring occasionally. Lift out the wool and stir Cream of Tartar into the dyebath. Dissolve a little Tin in a cup with some boiling water before adding it to the dyebath. Stir and put back the wool simmering for a further 20 minutes. Take out the wool and wash it in hot soapy water rinse and dry.

4.   Bright Green
*Method* Overdye wool dyed with indigo with the flowers and Alum. It gives a lovely bright green.

*Other uses*
Clan Badge of the MacLennans, Sinclairs and Logans
Used as a herb for wounds.

# 71. Wild Cress

*(Cardamine Flexuosa)*
*(Gael. Biolair)*

## GREATER BITTER CRESS

1.  Violet
A note given by Dr R. C. Maclagan on Highland Dyeing
1898 says: "Fancy here was seized upon the Gaelic name
Biolaire. This is a feminine noun, and in the nominantive
definite becomes a bhiolair (pronounced violair 'the violet').
Tests done gave the result as a nondescript grey."

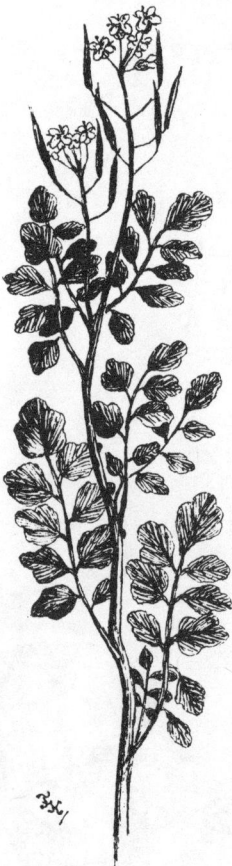

# 72. Wild Gean

*(Prunus Avium)*
*(Gael. Sirist)*

**WILD CHERRY**

1.   Cream – Tan
1lb bark to 1lb wool
*Method* Chop up the bark and soak, covering with cold water to be used for dyeing next day. Boil two hours and strain off the liquid into the dyebath. Cool to hand heat. Enter the wetted wool mordanted with Chrome. Simmer ½ hour for cream and longer for tan. Stir occasionally and remember to put a lid on. Lift out the wool and cool. Rinse and dry.

2.   Purplish Red
*Method* The root is said to give a purplish red. No mordant is mentioned.

# 73. Wild Hyacinth

*(Endymion non Scriptus)*
*(Gael. Fuath-Mhuc)*

**BLUEBELL**

**Flowers April to June. The Celtic Magazine of 1883
mentions Wild Hyacinth as giving a red dye.
No recipe is given but Hyacinth and the Rue are mentioned
and Hyacinth and Whortleberry as ingredients.**

*Other uses*
The roots were used for glue.

# 74. Willow

*(Salix atrocinerea)*
*(Gael. Seileach)*

## COMMON SALLOW

Charles Fergusson in "The Gaelic Names of Trees, Shrubs and Plants" 1878, says there were 16 varieties of Willows. Bark of most of the varieties was used to dye Black. No recipes are recorded. In present times, dyers use the leaves of most Willows to get Yellow with an Alum mordant. The bark, including osier strippings, gives from Gold to Orange, Red and Brown according to variety and using Alum and Chrome.

**WILLOW (WHITE) Grows on the west coast of Skye and occasionally on the west coast of Scotland.**

1.   Cinnamon – Flesh Colour
*Method* Recipe from Portree. Chop up the bark and soak overnight in the water to be used for dyeing. Boil next day for two hours, then pour off the liquid into the dyebath and cool to hand heat. Enter the wool mordanted with Chrome and simmer till required shade, stirring occasionally. Remember to put on the lid. Lift out the wool and cool. Rinse and dry.

*Other uses*
The old Highlanders found almost endless uses for Willow. The young twigs were made into baskets and even ropes. The bark was used for tanning. The foliage was enjoyed by cattle and horses, especially in autumn. Willows were valued greatly in the Hebrides, every twig being used for some purpose.

# 75. Yarrow

*(Achillea Millefolium)*
*(Gael. Lus na Fala)*

**A native perennial. Very common, on roadsides, disturbed ground and meadows.**

1.   Yellow
1lb plant tips to 1lb wool
*Method* Pick the tips of the plant while young, before coming into flower, and put them into the dyebath. Cover with cold water and enter the wetted wool mordanted with Alum and Cream of Tartar and push it down among the plant material. Simmer for ½ hour, stirring occasionally. Take out the wool and cool. Rinse and dry.

2.   Gold
*Method* As in recipe No. 1 but use Chrome mordant and remember to cover with a lid.

*Other uses*
Yarrow was used to stem the flow of blood. Also for treating headaches, the leaves being pushed up the nostrils until the blood sprung, from which very likely it took its Gaelic name of Lus na Fala, or the Blood Weed.
In 1777 Highlanders made an ointment of Yarrow to heal and dry wounds.
If going on a journey, it was the custom to kneel down and say with the right hand on the plant, "In the name of the Father and Son and Spirit journey prosper."

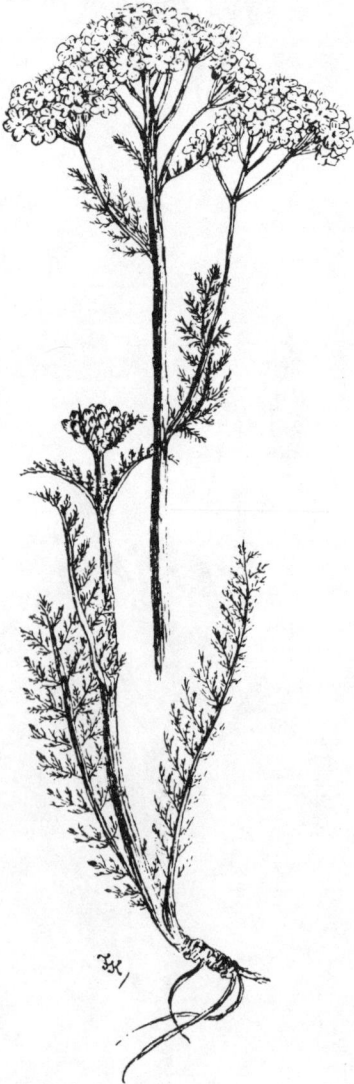

# BIBLIOGRAPHY

## Works referred to in the text

Bolton, Eileen, *Lichens for Vegetable Dyeing* (Studio Vista, 1963)

Brightman, Frank H., *The Oxford Book of Flowerless Plants* (Oxford University Press, 1966)

Campbell, Duncan, 'Highland Sheilings in the Olden Times', *Transactions of the Inverness Scientific Society and Field Club*, vol. 5 (1902), pp. 62–90

Cameron, John, *The Gaelic Names of Plants* (William Blackwood and Sons, 1883)

Carmichael, Alexander, *Carmina Gadelica* (*Ortha Nan Gaidheal*), 6 vols (1–5: Oliver and Boyd, 1928, 1928, 1940, 1941, 1954; 6: Scottish Academic Press, 1971)

Chambers, Robert, *Popular Rhymes of Scotland* (W. & R. Chambers, 1870)

Davenport, Elsie G., *Your Yarn Dyeing* (Sylvan Press, 1955)

Dunbar, John Telfer, *History of Highland Dress* (Oliver and Boyd, 1962)

Edmonston, Thomas, Jnr, 'Remarks on the Botany of Shetland', *Transactions of the Botanical Society*, vol. 1 (1844), pp. 185–88

Fairweather, Barbara, *Highland Plant Lore* (Glencoe and North Lorne Folk Museum, 1972)

Fergusson, Charles, *The Gaelic Names of Trees, Shrubs and Plants* (Inverness Free Press Printing and Publishing Co., 1878)

Grant, I. F., *Highland Folk Ways* (Routledge and Kegan Paul, 1961)

Grierson, Su, 'A Dyeing Art', *The Scots Magazine*, vol. 118 (Nov. 1982), pp. 124–31

Grieve, Mrs M., *A Modern Herbal* (Jonathan Cape Ltd, 1974)

Grigson, Geoffrey, *The Englishman's Flora* (Paladin, 1975)

Gunn, Rev. Adam, M.A. and John Mackay, eds, *Sutherland and the Reay County* (John Mackay, Glasgow, 1897)

'H', 'Celtic Dyes', *The Celtic Magazine*, vol. 8 (1883), pp. 211–12

Holden, Alexander Edward, *Plant Life in the Scottish Highlands* (Oliver and Boyd, 1952)

Kadans, Joseph M., *Encyclopaedia of Medicinal Herbs* (Thorsons, 1979)

Kok, Annette, 'A Short History of the Orchil Dyes', *The Lichenologist*, vol. 3 (1966), pp. 248–72

Lightfoot, John, A.M., *Flora Scotica*, 2 vols (B. White, London, 1777)

Lulham, R. B. J. and F. M. Haworth, *Lichens or Crottles (Special Leaflet no. 5)* (School Nature Study Union, 1935)

McClintock, H. F., *Old Irish and Highland Dress* (Dundalgan Press, 1943)

Mackay, J. G., *The Romantic Story of the Highland Garb and the Tartan* (Eneas MacKay, Stirling, 1925)

Maclagan, Dr R. C., 'On Highland Dyeing and Colourings of Native-made Tartans', *Transactions of the Royal Scottish Society of Arts*, vol. 14 (1898), pp. 386–410

Mairet, Ethel M., *Vegetable Dyes* (Faber and Faber, 1938)

Nicholas, Chris, 'The Use of Household Ammonia as a Colour Modifier in the Natural Dyeing of Wool', *Weavers Journal*, no. 99 (1976), pp. 11–12

Perring, F. H. and S. M. Walters, eds, *Atlas of the British Flora* (Thomas Nelson and Sons, 1962)

Phillips, Roger, *Wild Flowers of Britain* (Pan, 1977)

Robertson, Seonaid, *Dyes from Plants* (Van Nostrand Reinhold, 1973)

Ross, Donald Armstrong, *Plant Badges of the Clans* (Highland Information Pamphlet, 2nd series no. 23) (An Comunn Gaidhealach, Inverness, 1969)

Scott, Prof. W. R., *Home Industries Report* (Appendix 23) (HMSO, 1914)

Scottish Home Industries Association, *Scottish Home Industries* (Dingwall, 1895)

Shand, Winifred A., 'Dyeing Wool in the Outer Hebrides', *Dye Plants and Dyeing: A Handbook* (Brooklyn Botanic Garden, 1964), pp. 62–65

Shaw, Margaret Fay, *Folksongs and Folklore of South Uist* (Routledge and Kegan Paul, 1955)

Thompson, Francis, *Harris Tweed* (Highland Information Pamphlet no. 16) (An Comunn Gaidhealach, Inverness, 1969)

Thurstan, Violetta, *The Use of Vegetable Dyes* (Dryad Press, 1977)

Venables, Ursula, *Life in Shetland* (Oliver and Boyd, 1956)